A Ski Jumper's Life & Legacy

Gus Raaum

By Terry Murphy

A SKI JUMPER'S LIFE & LEGACY - GUS RAAUM.
Copyright © 2017 Lisbeth Raaum Harris
All rights reserved. No part of this book may be reproduced or transmitted in any form or by any means, electronic or mechanical, including photocopying, recording, or by an information storage & retrieval system, without written permission from the publisher.

Lisbeth Raaum Harris
PO Box 11341
Bozeman, MT 59719

Design: Lisbeth Raaum Harris
Photos: Courtesy of the Estate of Gustav F. Raaum

ISBN-10: 1975634993
ISBN-13: 978-1975634995

Prologue	5
Born To Ski	6
Christmas In Norway	17
The Calm Before The War	21
School Days	28
The End Of An Era	33
The End In Sight	44
The Germans Go Home	51
Jumping Into History	57
Cruising Into The Future	61
Part II	68
The American Letters	*68*
Shipping Out To Sea & Ski	70
The Bluest Skies In Seattle	79
North To Alaska (June 1947)	88
Sun Valley And Beyond	93
Smitten	99
The Land Of The Midnight Sun	103
A Job Well Done	110
My Girl	114
Love Is In The Air	118
Alaska By Sea	127
Torn Between Two Countries	133
A Season Of Joy	137
New Year, New Decade, New Life	143
Charging Ahead	148
June Was Busting Out All Over	152
The Fruits Of Labor	159
Yours Gustav 8/25/50	163

Part III 173
Two For The Road..*173*
Deportation Brewing 174
Big Steps & Baby Steps 179
Life Begins And Ends 184
Always An Adventure 190
Jackson Hole - The Next Frontier................196
The Sky's The Limit 205
Big Sky Country 211
Mountains Of Challenge 217
Chet & Gus 226
Goodbye Big Sky 234
Hello Seattle...238
Life Is Good 249
Royal Friendships 255
Joy & Loss 262
Olympic Memories..267
Beyond 70 And Going Strong 273
Full Circle..280
The Final Jump 285
Addendum.. 293

Prologue

For Gustav Raaum, every day was a good day, but March 3, 1946 had to be one of his best. On that day, more than 100,000 spectators, including the Norwegian Royal family, gathered at the Holmenkollen ski competition. It was the first competition in Holmenkollen since the end of World War II. All over Norway, people huddled by their radios, listening to the World Series of Ski Jumping.

In his own words, Gus said, "Every ski jumper's dream was to be able to compete in Holmenkoller." That dream was about to come true as Gus put on his skis and entered the start. Gazing down at the snowy woodlands, the crowds and that steep white run, little did Gus know he was about to plunge into world skiing history and become a national hero. That flight would land him on the Norwegian Ski Team and eventually into a new country *and* a new life.

This is a story about a Scandinavian immigrant who lived the American dream: a star athlete, a world-class education, and a successful business career. But for this humble man, what brought him the greatest pride was his wife, Claire, and the family they built together.

Chapter 1
Born To Ski

In the land of ice and timber, Brevik, Norway, Gustav Raaum "The Viking" made his entrance on January 20, 1926. As was the way then, a midwife was called to help his mother, Ingeborg, give birth. Sigurd, his proud father, was probably pacing somewhere in the house or at his soft goods store. Gus would join his older brother, Severin Fredrik "Dick" that day. Always the adventurer, when Gus was old

Ingeborg & Sigurd Raaum

enough to climb, he fell out of his crib, knocking himself unconscious. According to the story, their beloved housekeeper, Ruth Johnsen, came to his aid. Ruth would stay with the Raaum family throughout the years they lived in Nystrand. Later in his life, Gus described Ruth as, "A strong Christian and a wonderful person." The Raaum boys would be inseparable until years later when World War II tore entire families and countries apart. Dick would often say, no matter how far apart, "We were always close in spirit."

Gus had few memories of his grandparents except for his Grandmother Raaum, Hanna Andrea Schoubye "Amor". Amor lived until 1949. By then, Gus was in the United States. He never knew his fraternal grandfather Severin Fredrik Raaum who died 12 years before Gus was born. His maternal grandmother didn't live that long either. "My mother's mother, Marie Christina Petersen Christensen was born in Copenhagen, Denmark in 1859 and died in Skien on Feb. 4, 1933, when I was only 7 years old, so I do not have many memories of her."

Sigurd holding Gustav, 1926.

Gus was named after his maternal grandfather, Gustav Ferdinand Christensen who was a dentist in Skien. "My Grandfather Christensen was born on July 7, 1857 and died in Skien on April 20, 1928 when I was only 2 years old, so I do not remember him at all. He was a great sportsman and athlete." This would prove to be a good omen since Gus took after his Grandfather Christensen. Gus said of his grandfather, "He won many medals and awards. He competed in track and field, played soccer and was quite a gymnast. He was also president of the well-known sports club ODD in Skien." That inherited athletic prowess would set the stage for Gus's many accomplishments.

When Gus was born, the family lived in an apartment in Brevik. His brother Dick described it as being "…between the railroad and the docks." Their father and his four sisters had inherited a dry goods store in Brevik. Sigurd toiled for long hours at the store to support his family. After Gus came along, the apartment became too crowded for the family, so they moved to a lovely house in the village of Nystrand. (Nystrand means near the beach.) It was a small community out in the country at the end of Eidangerfjorden. Every day, Sigurd would commute by train to Brevik. His professional work ethic would lay a foundation for his two boys, and serve them well throughout their lives. According to Dick, their father gave both of them a gift that would last a lifetime. "He instilled in us the importance of being honest and responsible. And I think we were."

Gus, age 2

Gus and Dick enjoyed an idyllic childhood in Nystrand. Because they were close in age, they were each other's best friend. Looking back, Gus said, "We had a nice home where my brother and I shared a room. We had a beautiful garden which had over 100 varieties of roses." Dick also remembered the beautiful rose garden, their father's library and the maid's quarters. He also recalled lots of fruit trees: apple, plum and grey pear. The boys could eat fruit till their heart's and stomach's delight. Although Dick remembered much of the plum harvest going to waste as it all seemed to ripen at once. "Small yellow plums came in by the millions!" There was also a huge gravenstein apple tree that graced the front yard. Their mother would make lots of jam when the harvest came in.

The Raaum home in Nystrand.

It was a good-sized piece of property with a barn used for an ice house. There, Sigurd would store large blocks of ice in piles of sawdust. Because he hunted, he kept hunting dogs, and when they were old enough, he taught the boys how to shoot. Both brothers remember their father as being a very hard-working and caring father. Creating clouds of feathers, Dick and Gus would get into terrific pillow fights as children. (They quickly learned the real value of a vacuum cleaner.) Dick recalled a "noisy house" but he said they both "slept like logs." Together, they certainly learned to get into mischief. Both boys loved to play Cowboys & Indians in the forest where they would build their forts made of branches from fir trees. They fashioned pistols out of wood with a hole drilled for caps, an upside down nail head and a clothespin. According to Dick, their ammunition was "wads of paper."

That western theme was evident on Dick's sixth birthday. He received a cowboy outfit replete with a vest, a pair of chaps, kerchief, holster and a lasso. Two friends had arrived for the party, and Dick decided they needed to perform an act involving "saving the maiden." Well, the only available stand-in for a "maiden" was his little brother. From the second floor window, Dick decided to put the lasso around Gus's chest and lower him down to the ground. As little Gus was dangling in the air, Dick had a terrifying realization, "I didn't have enough of the rope." Dick hollered for their maid, Maggie who came running up the stairs.

Dick holding the lasso.

"Maggie, help, I can't get him back up!" Dick said. "Get who back up?" She asked. Once she realized four-year-old Gus was hanging out of the second story window, she let out a stream of expletives...then she saved the day by hauling Gus up. Later she dutifully told Dick's father what had happened while Dick braced himself for the worst.

Dick & Gus with Ajax, circa 1929.

Luckily his father said, "Dick, you can be glad it's your birthday today."

It's no surprise that their "cowboy" adventures were influenced by the movies they loved. Since the family had no car, occasionally the brothers would ride their bikes to the closest movie theater in a town called Porsgrunn. Their favorite movie stars were Tom Mix and Randolph Scott. Tom Mix was an American film actor who made hundreds of early western films between 1909 and 1935. (All but nine were silent.) Randolph Scott was also a western hero, known for his tall-in-the saddle roles. What a simple and wholesome pleasure the boys shared as they huddled in a dark theater, mesmerized by this slice of Americana. A few coins would buy a theater ticket, and maybe an extra treat as Gus recalled, "We got a few nickels from our parents to buy ice cream occasionally."

The family dog was a German Shepard named Ajax. Ajax was kept on a chain and, according to Gus, was quite intimidating. No one dared enter the garden when Ajax was on guard. When Ajax died, he was replaced by a Norwegian elkhound named Finn who apparently wasn't very popular with the neighbors since he would sneak into their yards and steal chickens. Fortunately, Gus and Dick kept their own rabbits safe in their cages.

In the summertime, the boys would swim and dive, fish, hike and play games. One of their favorite games was playing Tarzan. When Gus was nine, though, playing Tarzan turned out to be a painful experience. He was swinging from a rope that was too long and smashed his knee into a huge rock, slicing his kneecap open. Gus had to be carried home where the housekeeper/nanny reached his parents who called a doctor. When the doctor arrived, he was wearing a tuxedo and was quite inebriated having been called out of a party. Gus clearly remembered the doctor pouring iodine into the wound and promptly sewing him up without a drop of Novocain. A makeshift splint made from a wooden hangar (sans hooks) was strapped underneath Gus's injured leg. Even though he was laid up most of that summer, fortunately for Gus---and the sports world---he didn't end up with a permanent stiff knee. That marked the end of his career swinging from jungle vines.

Wintertime was as active as the warm weather months. The boys would go out to the farms and build their own snow hills for jumping. Their father started them skiing when Dick was only four and Gus was three. As they grew older, the boys would cut down a lot of birch trees to make their runs longer and harder. Gus recalled those carefree days when the seeds of competition were planted.

> While living in Nystrand I started to ski jump. The first time was when I was about 6 years old. As I approached the take-off I got scared and closed my eyes as I sailed over the take-off, then I fell on the landing. But from then on I got braver and continued to jump and improve. I trained hard and took part in competitions, some just with my brother and with my dad as judge in Kjempa hill. We got candy bars and sometimes honey cakes (which were sticky) as prizes. My dad gave me some very nice jumping skis and jumping bindings for Christmas.

Without any jealousy, Dick would say of his brother, "He was always better." Not only was Gus better, but he also avoided serious injury. Dick took a terrible fall as a youngster, and was in a coma for three days. After that, he never measured up to his brother's ability on the slopes.

Dick did find another winter sport he and Gus loved: a game called Bandy---or ball hockey--- on the frozen bay. Bandy is the forerunner to hockey and dates back 200 years. Even today, the sport is almost unknown on this continent, while in Norway, it is part of the national culture, drawing 30,000 fans to the annual championship. The game, a cross between field hockey and soccer, is extremely popular in small to medium-sized towns in Norway. Teams are comprised of eleven players. According to Gus, they used a stick similar, but lighter than a hockey stick to hit the ball.

Gus played several positions, including goalie. Each team had eleven boys gliding across the ice at high speeds. Of course, if you put boys wearing shape blades and traveling fast…accidents happen. Gus remembered one of those painful moments. He said, "One skater skated across my right thumb and the blade cut a nice scar near my thumbnail, putting me out of commission for a while." Fortunately, for Gus, it was only for a little while. He never stayed down for long.

Though, of all the sports Gus participated in, he loved ski-jumping the most. As the Chinese proverb says, "A journey of a thousand miles begins with a single step." That single step began the day Gus strapped on his skis for his first *real* competition. This is how he described that pivotal moment…a moment that would set the stage for the rest of his life.

> The first important ski jumping competition for me was near Porsgrunn when I was ten years old and I got 3rd place and won a very nice silver cup 1 ½ inches tall.

When I brought it home I put it on the edge of the mantle and told my mother and dad that every trophy I would win in the future would be bigger. This turned out to be true.

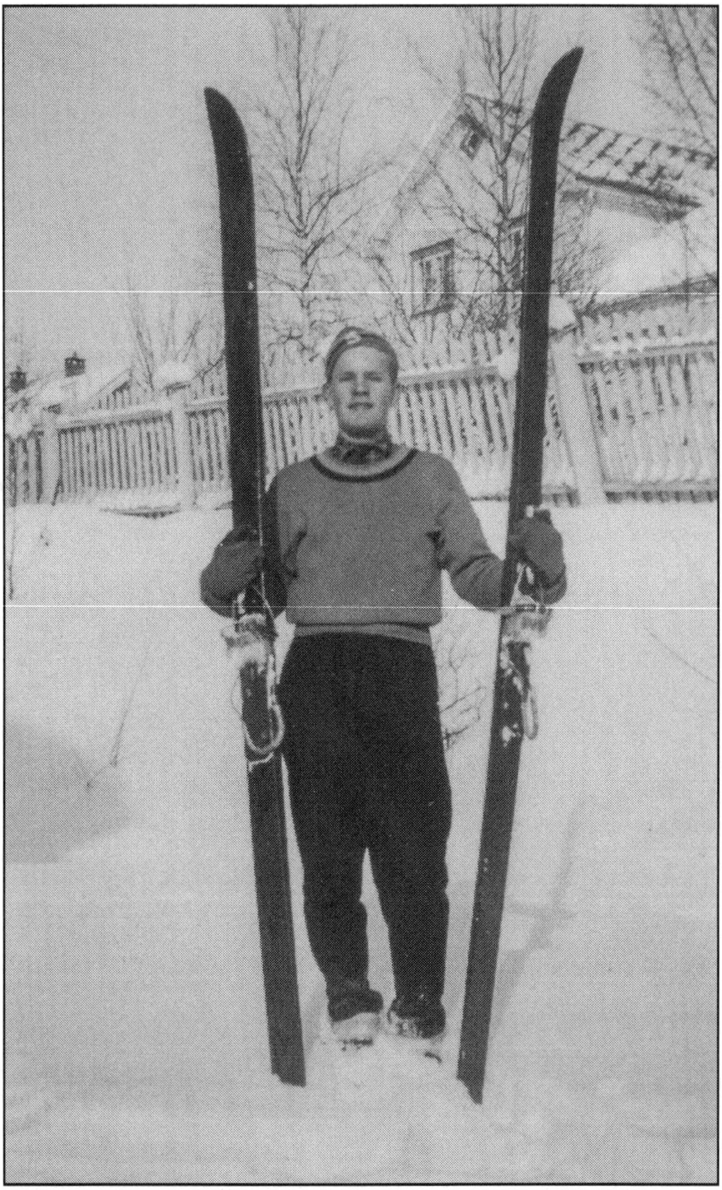

Chapter 2
Christmas In Norway

In Norway, Christmas is not just a day; it's a season lasting more than a month. This is not to extend the shopping season, but to make more time for holy days and festivities. Since the invention of electricity, the Norwegian holiday season (*juletid*) is a festival of light with a promise of longer days and the return of the sun. That promise is particularly important in Norway where noon can feel like twilight, and darkness closes in by 4 p.m.

As Gus recalled, "Christmas was a very special time of year." It was a time to be surrounded by family and friends. (It was also a time to practice his ski jumping.) As a young boy, Gus had especially fond memories of the Legaard family. Thomas Legaard who was a dentist gave Gus a cherished gift; his first pocket watch. Each year, the Raaum family would alternate Christmas dinner with the Legaard family.

Gus never forgot the wonderful Christmas spread that their families shared. Many were traditional holiday meat dishes: ribbe, a classic pork rib; spekekjott, a Norwegian delicacy of cured and dried lamb or mutton made best in late autumn; fenalaar, another kind of cured lamb; skinke (ham), rullepolse (rolled sausage) and svinekjott (pork). This was the time of year when the whole family could eat with great celerity. Tables groaned under the weight of prepared meats, lutefisk, various potato dishes, sauerkraut and more. Dinner would go on for hours.

Ingeborg Raaum and Ruth Legaard would bake Norwegian Christmas cookies for months ahead of time. Why so many cookies? Well, according to a Norwegian tradition, it's considered bad luck to serve less than seven types of cookies during Christmas-related events. Gus's recollection of *julfryd* or Christmas spirit was remembered in the cookies of his childhood. There were *Fattigmann* (poor man's cookie), fragrant of cardamom and brandy mixed together and deep fried in lard. *Berliner Kranser* (Berlin Wreathe) was a rich, delicate butter cookie. *Sandbakkels* were made best with European butter. *Krumkaker*, sometimes called waffle cookies, could be filled with whipped cream, berries or jam. *Pepperkaker* which means pepper cakes are the most commonly eaten Christmas cookie in Norway.

The day before Christmas Eve, the children were allowed to open one present and sample some of the holiday food. Gus recalled a small decorated tree being placed in the hall. But he and Dick were not allowed to see the tree before Christmas Eve. Behind the closed doors, their mother and Ruth would trim the main tree. (No peeking allowed.)

> We were not allowed to see the full Christmas tree before Christmas Eve. My mother and Ruth would decorate the tree, which was hidden in Dad's library,

and we were not allowed in the library. Ruth stayed in the house with another helper in a two-room apartment near Dad's library. These two rooms had a separate entrance, so the nannies could come and go without disturbing the family. We would also put up a small Christmas tree in the hall, and on the day before Christmas Eve we were allowed to open one present each, and to taste some of the food. Many of the Christmas tree decorations were homemade, and I helped to make some of them. On Christmas Eve we would all attend the children's church service from 4 to 5 PM. We would then come home and got a chance to see the big tree, and open presents.

Imagine the beauty of a snowy Christmas Eve in Norway. Family and friends hurry home after church service and gather in a warm, cozy home. Gus had clear memories of a wonderful Norwegian ritual, known as Circling the Christmas Tree. "We would walk around the Christmas tree holding hands and sing Christmas carols. The tree had real candles burning from top to bottom. For safety reasons my parents had both sand and buckets of water ready along the wall just in case." Afterwards, and much to the children's delight, gifts were distributed. Gus was always grateful for these cherished childhood memories. He would carry on many of these holiday traditions for the rest of his life. In fact, every Christmas season meant a trip to Ballard to stock up on Norwegian delicacies.

Those early holiday years in Gus's life were simpler times for his family and his country. Those memories of peace would sustain the Norwegian people through troubling times ahead. For the Raaum family, and all Norwegians, World War II loomed silently in the distant future, unseen and catastrophic. No one could have predicted that someday, the most famous Norwegian custom would be giving a Christmas tree to the UK every year. It would always be a gift to say thank you to the people of the UK who helped Norway during World War II. Each year, the tree stands in Trafalgar Square in the middle of London where hundreds come to see the lights turned on.

Chapter 3
The Calm Before The War

Life was good in Nystrand for many years, but in 1937 things started to change for the Raaum family. It began with problems around the family business. The family's soft-goods store was called "Severin F. Raaum" after Sigurd's father. Like most soft goods stores, Sigurd sold clothing, fabric, footwear, cosmetics, stationary and even medicines. Although Sigurd managed the store, he wasn't the sole owner; his four sisters, Herdis, Bibbi, Gunvor and Hanna were part owners. An unfortunate set of circumstances would cause bankruptcy and break family ties forever.

The first problem was that a large portion of blue collar workers in Brevik worked for Dalen Portland Cementfabrikk (a cement factory). Dick described this large factory as what "Boeing is to Seattle." The workers went on a two year strike; the length of the strike took a devastating toll. Of course, it greatly impacted Brevik's economy, including Sigurd's store. Then, to make matters worse, there was a fire in the store. Sigurd lost most of his inventory, and the final blow was that nothing was insured. To rebuild the stock, it would take capital, capital Sigurd didn't have. At that extremely inopportune moment, his four sisters demanded their shares of the store to be paid to them. Clearly, Sigurd couldn't meet their demands and the store was subsequently closed.

Sigurd's dream of someday passing the store on to his son, Dick, was crushed. A fact made worse in that, Dick had been named after Sigurd's father who established it. So much of Sigurd's life and legacy were tied up in the business. He'd made a comfortable living for his family and was well known in the community. To have it all ripped from him created a permanent riff between him and his sisters. Gus recalled how his father felt.

> My dad was very upset with his sisters for their demands while he was working his tail off to make the store a success. In fact, he was so upset he refused to have any contact with them for the rest of his life. The store's name was Severin F. Raaum and my brother was named after his grandpa. My dad's dream was to be able to hand the store over to my brother sometime in the future. When the store failed my dad broke down and asked my brother to forgive him for failing to save the store.

Nearly 80 years later, when asked about that time, Dick would say, "It was the only time I saw him cry." His father never really got over that sense of failure. "He was never the same." It would haunt Sigurd the rest of his life. Dick also recounted that his father was an honorable man. During the Dalen strike, "Dad had a book with the name of anybody on strike. He let them charge, and told them, "Pay me when you go back to work." Unfortunately, because the strike went on far longer than anyone ever imagined, that was impossible. But

The Raaum's home on Th. Lundesvei in Lillehammer.

once Sigurd secured a new job, he used part of his salary to pay people and "bank creditors" from his bankruptcy. Today, Dick still has dozens of "thank you letters" from grateful recipients.

In 1938, when Gus was twelve years old, his father took a job in Lillehammer. The family moved a few hundred miles north and started a new life. Dick recalled that, at first, the family stayed at a friend's summer house. Sigurd no longer owned but managed a similar but larger store called Th. Lunde on Main Street. According to Dick, their father would pay the boys 25 cents a week for allowance. Gus recalled living in several different homes, first north of Lillehammer and then near a church on Bjorstjerne Bjornson Street. Bjornson was a famous writer who won the Nobel Prize in Literature in 1903.

Eventually, they settled into a house at Th. Lundesvei which was owned by Ingeborg Raaum's brother, Christian Frederik Christensen. Probably, much to the boys delight their uncle (*onkel*) was a candy maker. They occupied the first floor and the basement of the house. A widow, Mrs. Kongsrud, rented the upstairs apartment. Her son, Haakon, was an artist, and Gus had a clear recollection of one of his sketches hanging on the wall of their home. The house had a beautiful view of Lake Mjosa; the largest and one of the deepest lakes in Norway and in Europe.

Gus, being a sociable young man, made lots of new friends in Lillehammer: Terje Hermanrud, Tore Mejdell, Jon Nilsen, Trout Grindal and Bodil Bjorklund. If the Bjorklund name sounds familiar, it's for good reason. Bodil's father, Thor, invented the famous Bjorklund cheese slicer in 1925. Even today, it's considered a classic symbol of Norwegian invention, quality and design.

Gus's lifelong passion for sports and the great outdoors continued after the move north. His best friend Kristian Syverud's grandfather had a marvelous log cabin with several out buildings in the mountains northeast from Lillehammer at Djupen. In all seasons, wonderful memories were made, whether it was spring, summer or deep into winter. One can only imagine the laughter echoing off the snowy fields and mountains as they made the journey through a winter wonderland. According to Gus, it would take an entire day to make the trip, sometimes struggling through wind and blizzards. They'd all arrive worn out, but knowing it was always worth it.

Gus & friends on their way to the cabin at Djupen.

In the winter there was no road to the cabin, so we had to pull a large sled full of all our food and luggage over the snow all the way into the cabin. This took all day and we arrived all worn out from this trip in, often fighting wind and snow blizzards. But we had a great time while there. In the summer time we would go fly-fishing on the lake nearby, we also built a diving board and had fun by the lake, and we hiked all over.

They would make the trek during Easter time, too, just in time to start working on a tan. "We spent many wonderful Easter and summer vacations there with other friends." As the weather warmed into summer, it was time to fly fish for trout at a spectacular Djupen mountain lake. And beyond water sports, there were hiking trips throughout the mountains and meadows. When they wanted to hike farther, they would pack rucksacks and tents for overnight adventures.

The mountains held all kinds of wholesome fun. Gus recalled helping out at mountain farms milking cows and churning goat milk into goat cheese. Another delightful treat was cloudberries (*Rubus chamaemorus*). Unlike blackberries or blueberries, these delicate amber-colored berries grow individually on a single stalk at ground level. As native plants, cloudberries are most characteristic of Scandinavia. These sturdy little plants thrive in the sub-Arctic landscapes of Norway, Sweden and Canada where they are called "bakeapples." Cloudberries can also be found in upper Minnesota. Intrepid foragers can find some *rare* patches in Washington State---the place where Gus would one day live. These berries are prized in Scandinavia but don't lend themselves to commercial cultivation. Therefore, gatherers keep the location of their patches secret…adding more to their mystique.

In that time of youth and innocence or "salad days," as Shakespeare called them, Gus and his buddies could eat cloudberries without a care in their hearts. But beyond the mountains and over the horizon, the seeds of war were being sown. Even after the German invasion the winds of war would change Norway forever, but the mountains would still offer Gus refuge. "One summer (during the occupation) with our friends we took a long 2-week hiking trip through Jotunheimen where there are numerous hiking trails. We packed everything we needed in our rucksacks and stayed in our tent. We climbed to the top of Glittertind and Galhopiggen, the highest mountain tops in Norway."

Throughout the rest of Gus Raaum's life, the mountains and his love for outdoor sports would shape his future, and make athletic history.

Chapter 4
School Days

The Lillehammer boys gymnastics team. Gus is at far right.

When it came to sports, high school was a formative time for Gus. As he would later say, "We were encouraged to participate and stay in shape." He competed in soccer in the center half defense position. He garnered medals in track in various events including high jump, long jump and the 60 yard dash. Gus also participated in gymnastics with trampoline, pommel horse, rings and tumbling. All these sports were building an athletic specimen with tremendous upper and lower body strength. This didn't leave a lot of time for Bandy, but he still engaged in speed skating. With a myriad of sports, though, Gus always pursued his first love, ski jumping. As he developed his body, Gus also developed his mind. Academics were arduous, and given the choice of studying math, physics or language, Gus chose math and physics. The Norwegian school system was particularly challenging because students were tested on everything at the end of school; no semesters or quarters in those days. As in many European countries, English was taught. For Gus, it began in the last two years of grade school and continued throughout high school. But English was only one of a few languages that were taught. Old Norwegian, which Gus described as "almost Icelandic," was one of them. Old Norwegian was spoken between the 11th and 14th centuries. After the plague or "Black Death," the language of Norway changed between 1350 and 1550 which is referred to as Middle Norwegian.

Beyond that, students were required to study one year of French and four full years of German. English was always considered the second language, until the German invasion. For Gus and his fellow students, that added more hardship. "After the Germans occupied Norway we were forced to concentrate on the German language as more important than English (which was always our 2nd language). All the schools were serious and we had to study hard. The hard part was that at the end of a full year we had to take exams on all the material we had studied during the whole year, no quarter or semester system."

Once the German occupation took place, it infiltrated the entire school curriculum. The German army occupied the schools, and according to Gus, "Arrested many of the school principals who refused to instruct according to German mandate." As in many things that went underground, so did education. Many students attended school in private homes to get out from under the German fist.

To keep spirits up, Gus would watch his parents play Bridge. Sure enough, he learned to play proficiently even entering competitions. Bridge would also be an outlet during the occupation because people's movements were restricted. "I ended up playing a lot of bridge, and with a long time partner I entered bridge competitions. This was particularly so during the German occupation when we were pretty much restricted with what we could do."

In the evenings, once the boys finished their homework, they could listen to the radio. In that era, it was called the Golden Age of Radio. Not only was there popular music, but many radio dramas that kept listeners on the edge of their seats with mystery, adventure and detective series. Of course, radio kept the listeners apprised of what was going on globally and in their own backyards.

The Raaum family was fortunate to get one of the first refrigerators in Lillehammer. Prior to then, a large block of ice kept food fresh. Early on, Gus and Dick developed a work ethic. The following recollection would be a parent's dream for their child: "My brother and I had to do housework such as dusting, vacuum, wash and dry dishes, and outside chop and split fire wood, and pick fruit when the different fruits were ripe."

But those simple days would soon be a memory for the Raaums and their country. The world was changing in a profound and painful way. On November 30, 1939, the USSR attacked Finland. The Red Army crossed the Soviet-Finnish border with 465,000 men and 1,000 aircraft and bombed Helsinki. The Lillehammer Ski Club organized a jumping competition to collect money for the benefit of Finland. At the age of 13, Gus and his Norwegian counterparts joined top jumpers from Finland to take part in the competition. After Finland put up a mighty fight, the conflict between the USSR and Finland ended March 13, 1940 with the Moscow Peace Treaty. Only a month later, the German Army would be invading Norway. Throughout that time, Gus never gave up his ski jumping or his resistance to the enemy.

Gus & Dick harvesting apples.

Chapter 5
The End Of An Era

The Nazi army marches into Lillehammer, 1940.

Gus never forgot the day everything changed: "On April 9, 1940 the German army invaded Norway and occupied Norway until May 8, 1945. This changed our lives drastically." Gus was only 14 when the occupation began. Norway had maintained a position of neutrality, but on the pretext that Norway needed protection from British and French interference, Germany invaded. Of course, Germany had more self-serving motives. They wanted to secure ice-free harbors from which their navy could control the north Atlantic. There were also iron ore mines in Sweden that went through Narvik. According to Dick Raaum, the Germans were also jealous; they believed that Norwegians were "The closest to pure Arians in the world." Norway would be one more jewel in the German empire's crown. Gus proudly said of that defeat, "While Denmark and Holland fell in one day, and France fell in three weeks, it took the Germans two months to defeat an undermanned Norwegian force." British forces came to help, but they proved to be unreliable and ineffective.

Oslo fell very soon. The first troops to enter Oslo had the audacity to march behind a German brass band. Fortunately, the royal family escaped by ship and took refuge in England. Dick remembered June 7, 1940 very clearly because it was his birthday, "The royal heads of Norway were picked up by an English cruiser."

The Norwegian government asked for volunteers to join the armed forces as the German troops advanced north toward Lillehammer. But the effort was doomed to fail. As Gus recalled, "Norway was very poorly prepared for defense of its country. The surprise attack on Norway caused us to lose most of the few fighter planes we had. But the army mobilized the best they could." Because Dick was older than Gus, he remembered more details. For instance, when the British and French tried to defend Norway, "They [the Germans] didn't meet much opposition. Lillehammer was easy to take, an open city. The English and French had been sent over. The French were not dressed properly." Dick goes on to say, it was very cold, that

French and English troops wore light uniforms, and the French wore, "dancing shoes."

The major Norwegian ports from Oslo northward to Narvik were occupied by advance detachments of German troops. After establishing footholds in Oslo and Trondheim, the Germans launched a ground offensive against scattered resistance inland. But the Norwegians were no match for the German forces. As the troops advanced toward Lillehammer, Gus and Dick decided they would get a rifle, shells and an armband. (They had no uniforms.) As volunteers, they wanted to be hauled in a pick-up truck south toward the advancing German army. But their father got wind of what the boys were planning and foiled it. He rushed to the town square and told them they were too young and forbid them to go. Gus recalled a doomed effort by volunteers to slow the troops with felled trees. German tanks simply rolled right over the trees.

Gus couldn't join the forces, but he could help out. He joined the Red Cross forces and helped carry wounded soldiers from ambulances to the temporary hospital set-up in the high school gymnasium. All the while, the Germans relentlessly would strafe his town with machine gun fire and drop bombs as the German troops advanced by ground. The British Broadcasting Corporation (BBC) was a pipeline on the progress of the War, but eventually all radios were confiscated. After that, news came from the underground.

Things went from bad to worse as the German army established its headquarters at the outskirts of Lillehammer. Gus believed there were more German soldiers---approximately 20,000---than Norwegian citizens. He recalled the Germans proclaiming they came to Norway to "Save us from the British." He and his comrades found that laughable, while the Germans tried to feign camaraderie. The Norwegians froze the Germans out, but then they and their Norwegian turncoats would seek their revenge; confiscating all radios and guns, requiring ID cards and restricting travel. Decent food and materials were taken away and used for the German war effort. Very strict rationing of food and materials was enforced. Like the Irish, potatoes became the mainstay of their diets. Gus described eating lots of potatoes, which they used as sandwich spread, then fried and cooked and mashed for dinner. Another food that was available was blood pudding and blood sausage which is usually made from pork blood. Gus found it repulsive and swore if he made it through the war; he would never eat it again. He stuck to his word. They had meat only once a month. Gus recalled that the Germans were particularly interested in butter, he said, "Since they used it in the process to make glycerin explosives." He also speculated that Germans had generally "poor eyesight due to lack of certain vitamins in their diet, so they were poor in aiming and hitting their targets with their guns." Imported fruit, such as bananas, pineapples, oranges were an absolute luxury. So many of what we take for granted today was completely out-of-reach. But once again, through luck and guts, Gus and his family found a way around this.

> Fortunately my dad knew many farmers who were customers of the store, so we had opportunities to get some meat from farmers, which was illegal. We would have been arrested, and put in jail, in addition to losing the meat. Occasionally I would go on my bicycle up the valley to a farm to pick up some meat, which I put in the special side bags on the bicycle. Occasionally we would run across a German roadblock which would check people's identification and see if they had any illegal products in their possession. When we saw the roadblock up ahead, we would circle back and find a dirt side road up on the hillside to avoid them.

At first, Gus believed the Germans were "outgunned" by the Norwegian soldiers, so they paid dearly in lives for their invasion and occupation of Norway. The Germans were determined to completely isolate the Norwegians. Under severe penalty and/or jail, the Germans required everyone to turn in their radios; cutting off all contact with the outside world. But as always, ingenuity and subterfuge won the day. The Raaum's neighbor, Mr. Bjorklund (inventor of the famous cheese cutter "SPAR") hid one good radio behind a basement wall. It was wired by hooking it up to two metal coat hanger hooks with a listening device. They were then able to tune in the BBC on short wave radio. According to Gus, "They took down the details of the news, made copies, which were distributed around town through an underground network. This often consisted of small children with the usual rucksack, which the children used to carry their lunch and books to school."

But the Germans always had their ways of rooting out their enemy. They had listening equipment which they used to trace and locate illegal radios. Realizing something was amiss in the Raaum neighborhood, they went on a house-to-house search, banging on every door. Then one early morning, the German soldiers finally zeroed in on the Bjorklund home. As they pounded on the door, the two older Bjorklund brothers jumped out of bed---still in their pajamas--fled through the back door out into the snow. According to Gus, they got away, crossed the border to Sweden and were eventually shipped to England to join the Norwegian liberation forces there. Sadly, though, another neighbor, Helge Froysland, was not so lucky. Froysland was double-crossed by a turncoat who divulged his hiding place. As he tried to flee the Germans, Froysland was shot in the back. The German Army meant business, and would not hesitate executing anyone who dared to defy orders.

For the most part, Gus and all his friends would ignore the German soldiers as they moved about Lillehammer. If they spotted a Norwegian girl socializing with any of the German soldiers, she, too, would then be ignored or as Gus put it, "frozen out." From Gus's recollections, very few Norwegians joined the Nazi party. The German's puppet Norwegian government was headed by Vidkun Quisling, who, incidentally, had been his mother's history teacher at a school in Skien. The greatest danger of living alongside the "turncoats" was if a Norwegian were traveling on a false passport, the traitor would recognize them and had the ability to turn them in.

During the occupation, Norwegian underground groups dared to sabotage certain buildings and bridges. There were efforts to eliminate certain "very bad" Gestapo or Nazi turncoats. To fight back, the Gestapo would arrest ten prominent (often innocent) citizens of a town early in the morning. They would drag these poor souls to the town square and shoot them down in cold blood. This was a clear warning to anyone who had the slightest urge to sabotage the German war effort.

Gus and his family were forbidden to travel outside the area without a permit. To keep busy, he and Dick joined a sail gliding club. He recalls that Major Solberg, who later became a general, was in charge of the club. Being the daredevils they were, Gus and Dick decided to build their own sailplane in the garage. Unfortunately, a German who was born and reared in Norway prior to the occupation took it upon himself to report them. The German army was swift to confiscate the sailplane, never to be seen again. Undeterred, Gus and his friends continued their sail club. It proved to be a training ground for the members; Rolf Bentsen would go on to fly fighter planes for the Norwegian forces in England. Some flew to even greater heights: members, Roar Holmen and Gunnar Berge, ended up in charge of the Norwegian Air Force in England.

Eventually, the young men built a "school glider" at Jorstadmoen which was north of Lillehammer. Their first disastrous move was the Aero Club getting tan and orange caps. Turned out, these were the same colors of the Nazi's, so they were quickly discarded. When they finally were able to try out the glider plane, it was quite a production. The pilot seat was solid wood, no cushioning at all. The men dragged the plane out to an open sloping field on a farm. According to Gus, the test was done by using a large piece of elastic rope that was hooked in the nose of the plane. Then several men would run out in front of the plane to tighten the elastic rope. Meanwhile, several men held the tail of the plane. Once they released the plane, the idea was to catapult it like a slingshot. If things went well, the plane would fly straight and in balance. But this is how Gus described his first ride:

> I was strapped in the wooden straight back seat. When it was my turn and the plane was turned loose I made the mistake of pulling the stick back, so the plane lifted (unintentionally) off the ground just for a few seconds but it felt like minutes. I had actually flown solo for a few seconds on my first try. I landed with a big bang,

and the head of the club was not too pleased since I could have ruined the plane.

Fortunately, Gus was free to move around to some extent. He had a fond memory of a summer bicycle trip with his friend, Kristian Syverud. They pedaled from Lillehammer to Oslo which was 125 miles. They packed a hardy lunch and plenty of water. Gus also started to learn how to play tennis even though there were no coaching lessons. These were a few of his good memories at a time when his country was torn apart by strife.

Gus also had clear recollections that during the German occupation, most mail was intercepted by Nazi government workers who censured letters. In the following letter (Feb. 13, 1941) his mother wrote to their former housemaid, Ruth, she's careful to keep the content fairly general, saying, "There is a lot to report, but that has to wait until another time."

Here are some of Gus's mother's comments:

> "I was happy to read that you came back home during this anxious time. What can we say about all this tragedy which now weighs upon Norway? It is all unbelievable, but we have to keep a cool head and hope. There is a lot to report, but that has to wait until another time. Mr. Raaum likes his new job, but there is quite a bit of responsibility when you are in charge of

such a large store. Unfortunately Mr. Raaum has been very sick. It is unbelievable for he has always been so strong and healthy, but he scared himself and us quite a bit. He had a lot of blood in his stomach, ulcer, and he has been in bed for a quite a while. In addition he has had 5 operations for hemorrhoids which has bothered him a lot. The boys are big now, and they are really enjoying the snow and skiing. Gustav is extra interested in ski jumping and won several trophies last year. This year has put a damper on such activities, but it will come back. He is expecting 1st prize next Sunday in the school ski jumping tournament. Time will show. Dick also jumps a little, but he is not as good. Otherwise they are working hard in school. Dick shall take his middle school exams this summer. He took the 1. Class over again, so he would not appear stupid when we arrived here. The boys lost 2 ½ months of schooling as we moved here to Lillehammer. The boys help me a lot and they are very good at it. In April I laid off Reidun, since we only received ¾ pay, and lately I have managed with help every Friday. For a while I went without any help. Can you imagine me up and at them at 7:30 AM? We are living a quiet life, and it is nice to be busy, since we don't have to think about all the other problems. I am often very tired, and this period has been very tough for me. In the meantime the boys are growing, and they cost more to keep. The prices here compared to Nystrand, where we came from, everything here is much more expensive. And it is so terribly cold here, 8 months of winter and 4 of them very cold, so electricity requires lots of money. Can you remember how I hated the winter season? The irony is that we have ended up here in the cold country. We are now living in a nice house, we have the 1st floor and the basement and the attic, 4 rooms, shower, sink with warm and cold water and toilet and kitchen, and a small maid's' quarters in the attic. The boy's bedroom is heated by expensive electricity. We have a very nice bathroom with a bathtub in the basement. We have a beautiful view, but we were a "target" in the spring, but everything went OK, nobody had to be evacuated. The family stayed together, so we were not separated." (End of letter)

Clearly, Ingeborg Raaum was doing her best to share the challenges of their life, but doing it, in a way that won't get the family in trouble. These hardships would go on for years as the Germans continued their reign of terror.

Gus & friend Kristian Syverud on their Oslo bicycle trip.

Chapter 6
The End In Sight

When the German troops took over Lillehammer, Dick was furious as armed Norwegians did nothing. "They [Germans] just walked and marched through. They all had their weapons, but nobody shot at them." Dick asked himself, "Why in heck am I not fighting them?" But living alongside enemy troops put all Norwegians in peril. Gus recalled a group of Norwegians who hid hand grenades, ammunition, and guns. Unfortunately, the Germans confiscated most of them. But Gus's brother was a clever young man. Somehow Dick got his hands on a revolver, three bullets and a completely new barrel. He hid all of it under an out-building next to their Lillehammer home. At sixteen, still determined to fight, Dick did his best to join the Norwegian resistance. He lied, and said he was eighteen-years-old. His father came to the rescue again, and found Dick at the railroad station ready to take a uniform and weapons. His father "chewed out the Captain" for taking a boy who was not of age. Dick recalled, "I cried" when he missed this chance to serve.

At that time, the Swedish Prime Minister, Christian Guther, allowed the Germans to travel in closed railroad cars through Norway to the harbor. Because Guther was sympathetic to the Germans during the War, he was thrown out of office in the next election. Even though there's not much historical information as to why, but according to

Gus, Norwegian troops trained in Sweden were nicknamed "Lumberjacks."

At the age of 18, the Nazis drafted Norwegian youngsters. Gus recounted how his brother, Dick, was arrested and taken to a labor camp where he was forced to help Nazi sympathizers and farmers by digging ditches. Sixteen young men slept in barracks, and returned each night after a hard day's work. Dick was in camp from May to October in 1944 as the Germans started to lose the war. Gus recounted that his brother was regularly beaten.

Before Dick was arrested, he and Gus worked at "Vengshoel's farm" in Gausdal, north of Lillehammer. (Their father wanted them out of the city and in the safety of the country). The boys stayed for 2 ½ months and worked 6 full days; cleaning stalls for cows and horses, threshing, bailing hay, planting and harvesting potatoes, and maintaining the entire vegetable garden. At the end of the season, Gus says he received "forty-five kroner which was equivalent to $7." When Gus and Dick first arrived at the farm, they were considered "city boys" or sissies by the local farm workers. To prove their bravery, they both did a high dive off a bridge into a deep water hole of a local river. After that, they were one of the gang.

During this time, there were about 20,000 German troops in their army headquarters near Lillehammer. The Germans also established two large concentration camps outside Lillehammer to house Russian prisoners of war. The Germans were brutal to them, many died of torture and starvation. It was required for Gus's high school class to show up for labor camp. Many of the boys met secretly in the woods near a swimming lake at Stampesletta. Together, they decided to defy the Nazis and not report to the labor registration office. Gus never forgot what happened next. It not only changed the course of his life, but probably saved it.

> Several days later one of the German officials showed up at our house looking for me. My mother answered the door, and told them I was not in, (which was a lie) they told her I better show up by 5 PM to report. I was hiding at home at that time and then immediately took my ryggsack (rucksack) full of my most essential clothes and headed to a farm south of Lillehammer where I stayed in hiding until the Germans got too busy losing the war. I learned to milk cows and did general work around the farm. One day 2 German soldiers approached the farm and when I saw them coming I thought they were after me, so I hid underneath a bed up on the second floor. It turned out that they were thirsty and wanted some milk, but in the meantime my heart was pounding. The farm was owned by Mr. Gulsvik who was a CPA and whose youngest daughter was my girlfriend, Bjorg Gulsvik.

While working on a different farm, Dick supplied subversive newsletters at Stampesletta. (Today, the new hockey stadium stands in its place.) The day Dick was arrested at Vengshoel's farm, he was out in the fields shoveling manure. He described his arrest this way: The German officer approached and said in German "Come over here. You are to come with us." Because Dick reeked of manure, they allowed him to change his clothes. He was taken in a black car to Gestapo headquarters and interrogated by Gestapo for more than three hours. On the way there, though, Dick tells a poignant story. He said he saw his mother standing on a bridge as the black car passed. She could see Dick in the car. He said, "She looked pretty sad. She didn't know what would happen. She maybe thought I would be shot." This scene was replayed all over Norway, as mothers and fathers watched their sons be hauled away by German forces. During this time, Dick said he had no idea where his brother was, nor did he want to know. That way, he could tell the truth when asked, "Where is your brother?"

The Gestapo found 23 young men who testified that Dick had attended a resistance meeting, and that he had also distributed anti-Nazi information. A 6' 8" Gestapo named Kimmel hit Dick, and asked him, "Who will win the war?" Dick answered, the Germans would lose. They slapped him around. When they asked him again, who would win the war, he said, the United States. (The U.S. wasn't involved yet, but, of course, this further infuriated his interrogator.) "Then, they *really* slapped me." They asked him who his contact was, and he said he didn't have one. To make matters worse, a druggist named Grundtvig was brought in and he told the Gestapo that Dick had distributed treasonous information.

Dick was thrown into the Police Headquarters in Lillehammer, and from there to labor camp in Biri, south of Lillehammer. One saving grace was that Dick spoke fluent German. The Gestapo asked him where he learned the language, and he told them in school, and that he had read "Das Boot." There were a total of about 120 people in the camp. For his birthday, June 7, 1944, Dick was allowed to leave the camp with two sergeants to pick up mail and supplies. He picked up a stack of newspapers, and the headline said, "Allies Land in Normandy." He said to himself, "My God, this is about over!" When he returned to the camp, he placed the stack on the Commandant's desk, with the headlines carefully turned toward him. Dick declared, "You have had it." This act of insolence earned Dick two weeks in the "the cooler." Dick described time spent in the brig as, "The best thing was because nobody else in the camp knew, but I knew." The end was near, but until that happened, the men were sent out to dig ditches for irrigation. Now with liberation on the horizon, Dick described the ditches as "beautiful" because the diggers purposely dug as slowly as possible.

As the war went on, so did Gus's passion for ski jumping. During the winter, Gus trained hard with his ski jumping, taking part in "secret" ski jumping competitions. If the Germans attempted to organize any competitions, the "true Norwegians" went on strike. Instead, Gus says they organized "illegal competitions around the district." In 1945, a big secret competition took place in Lismarka, outside Lillehammer. Among many competitors, fifteen jumpers from the Oslo area somehow obtained travel permits to Lillehammer. Gus recalled a joyous occasion that turned ugly. "After the competition we had a big award ceremony party at Strand restaurant. However, Gestapo showed up at this function and arrested four competitors who went to the Gestapo jail at Suttestadjordet."

None of this stopped Gus and his ski buddies from pursuing what they loved most. The "Skarp" club held more secret competitions and often trained near Lismarka. With their skis on their shoulders, and food and wax in their heavy rucksacks, the men trudged over the mountain to Lismarka. How brave these men were, willing to risk their very lives to keep their dreams alive. Once they reached their destination, preparing a place was also arduous. "Then we had to prepare the hill by foot tramping the snow, then, smooth it out with ski packing. We had to hike from the outrun to the top of the start to take maybe 5 or 6 jumps before it got dark, then we had to walk about 2 hours to get back home."

The Germans were determined to confiscate the Lillehammer Ski Club's books, but Gus's friend, Charles Winquist --who headed the club during the war years--hid them. Gus never forgot his other friends who did well: Harald Mathisen, Nils Laursen and Odd Johansen. During this time, Gus worked part-time at a bow and arrow factory with Frank Waastad Olsen and Odd Winquist.

Gus at Lismarka ski jump, circa 1945.

As the war started to wind down, Gus and his cohorts could identify specific "turncoats" whose actions and sympathy for the Germans made life miserable for their population. They had decided that when the war ended, they would "put them through hell and execute them." But then they learned from their Government in exile that many of the people they had pinpointed were actually double agents. And these double agents had lived through hell to provide the Norwegians with critical information during the occupation. Fortunately, they did not make the mistake of torturing or executing the wrong men, an error that would have carried a lifelong regret.

Chapter 7
The Germans Go Home

Finally, after five years of German occupation, the glorious day arrived; on May 8, 1945 the War was over! Gus remembered that the transfer of power to the Norwegian people and the Norwegian underground "went very smoothly." Fortunately, the underground troops were well armed and trained. Gus described his immediate experience once the war ended:

> I went on guard duty at the German / Russian concentration camp at the outset to keep order between Germans and Russians, and later I was on guard duty where we held turncoat prisoners before they could be brought to trial. I had only a Colt 45 handgun in my belt for security. I was 19 years old then. Except for a very few acquaintances who were shot, most of my friends survived. My dad developed an ulcer and had to be hospitalized for treatment and he escaped otherwise unharmed. My brother returned from labor camp with a few scars and bruises, but also survived OK.

Dick was still in the camp when the war was beginning to end. He said that morning there was no revelry. The soldiers got up in the silence, dressed and went outside. There were no officers around. Dick suggested they go over to the headquarters and they found not a single person there. Then, he noticed a telephone on the commandant's desk. He picked it up and called his mother. He said, "We need someone to take us out of this place. And she said what are you talking about? I said every officer has left…every one of them." He went on to tell his mother that there were about 60 prisoners who need transportation. (A few had already left on foot.) Then, he spoke with his father who arranged to get a friend with a truck. They packed it up with P.O.W.'s and took off for Lillehammer. "What a day," is how Dick described it. They had to hide the truck behind a store because there were still some Germans lurking in the city and the mountains.

Life was still very difficult after the war was over. In large cities such as Oslo, Bergen and Trondheim, food shortages were severe. Families would stash a lot of canned food in woodpiles. One item, sardines, was particularly coveted because it is high in vital nutrients; vitamin D and olive oil. Harder to come by were cigarettes and tobacco. Gus recalled trying to grow tobacco in their garden but, "It tasted terrible." No doubt. And even though it's unfit for human consumption, Gus said, "We also tried to boil denatured alcohol to make it edible, but this was also very unsuccessful."

Gus finished his high school math and chemistry exams in 1944. Always a conscientious student, he decided to take his senior year over to improve his grades in order to get into a good university. He felt his education during the war was short-changed because classes were held in semi-secret outside the main school buildings. When it was time to graduate, Gus described some very fond memories:

> The graduating class always wore red caps with a tassel and we carried a small bamboo stick with a ribbon. Tor Mejdell and I were put in charge of planning a fun event in Oslo to celebrate our graduation, so we went to Oslo and were able to line up one evening of entertainment including the Leif Juster show at Chat Noir Theatre. We had to agree to take the whole theater and since our class was not large enough to fill up the theater, Tore and I had to run up and down Carl Johans Street, the main street, in Oslo trying to sell enough tickets to sell out the theater, otherwise our class had to come up with the shortage. It finally worked out.

In Lillehammer, the Raaum family lived near a very famous writer named Sigrid Undset. She was a fascinating woman with quite a life story. Undset was born in Denmark, but moved to Norway when she was two-years-old. At the age of 25, she would make her literary debut with a scandalous novel called "Fru Marta Oulie." Undset was granted a writer's scholarship and she traveled all over Europe. In 1919, she moved back to Lillehammer, and after her marriage ended, she wrote her masterpiece. Between 1920 and 1927, she first published the 3-volume *Kristin Lavrandatter* and then the 4-volume *Olav* which was translated into English as *The Master of Hestviken*. In 1940, when the Germans invaded Norway, Undset fled the country. She had strongly criticized Hitler and her books were banned in Germany. Fearing imprisonment by the Nazis, she escaped to neutral Sweden. Her eldest son was killed in action only a few kilometers from their home at Bjerkebaek. During the occupation, her home was occupied by the German army and used as the officers' quarters. Undset left Sweden and took her younger son to America where in her writings, interviews and speeches she pleaded her country's cause, and that of the Jews.

In 1945, after the occupation ended, Undset returned to Norway. She was described as "exhausted" and never wrote another word. She would die only four years later at the age of 67 in Lillehammer. Sigrid Undset was honored in many prestigious ways: she won the Nobel Prize for literature; a crater on Venus is named for her; she's been depicted on Norwegian currency; and on a postage stamp from 1982. In 1998, Sweden honored her with a stamp. Her home in Lillehammer, Bjerkebaek, is part of the Maihaugen museum.

In Gus's recollections, it's interesting to read his impressions of this world famous woman:

> In Lillehammer we lived near Sigrid Undset who lived in a log home. She won the Nobel Prize for literature. She was a real odd person, very private and kept to herself. I have her series of books (10 volumes) which

are all autographed by the author. I inherited these from my parents. In March 1999 I donated these books to the University of Washington, where they are located in the Special Collection section of Suzzallo Library. These books can be viewed and read in the Library, but cannot be checked out.

Undset's books were not the only priceless thing Gus would inherit. Because of its fresh air and beauty, Lillehammer attracted many artists. Gus's father befriended many of these artistic folks and he began to buy and collect oil paintings, prints and books. Because the department store he managed carried unique hand-crafted furniture, he had gorgeous furniture crafted for the Raaum home. The store also had the sole right to copy furniture, which was displayed, at Maihaugen Museum at Lillehammer, a huge outdoor museum area with houses, out buildings and personal property and tools, some close to 1,000 years old. Gus and his brother Dick would one day inherit this furniture and many of the paintings which would grace their homes. There was also a treasure trove of silver, Rosenthal dishes, crystal and jewelry. A precious gold pocket watch and chain that Gus inherited from his grandfather Christensen would one day be passed on to Gus's grandson, Erik; his name already was engraved on the inside cover.

The Raaum brothers were separated at the beginning of the war, and would remain so for a long time. Dick went off to Sweden to work, while Gus rose in the ranks as a champion in the sport of ski jumping. Decades later, Dick recalled that when Gus married in the U.S., he sent the family in Norway an audio recording of his wedding on a record to play on a turntable. Gus also sent a piece of wedding cake. With a smile on his face, Dick described it as, "It was the driest piece of cake you ever saw."

The brothers, who Dick said, "Never had a fight," would one day meet again on American soil, but many things would happen before then.

Ready for guard duty.

Chapter 8
Jumping Into History

The training Gus did before and during the War started to pay off for him and his friends. Gus Raaum, Frank Waastad Olsen, and Odd Winquist made headlines in the sports world: "Aggressive Recruits." That article went on to say, "Junior jumpers at Lillehammer are a new skiing power among our ski jumpers." Then they added: "Will Lillehammer become another Kongsberg?" Kongsberg---a mecca for skiers---translates to Kong, meaning King, as in King Christian, and Berg, which means mountain. Kongsberg was founded in 1624, and named for Danish-Norwegian king Christian IV, as a silver mining community. Later, it would be known for its silvery slopes where world champion ski jumpers would compete.

In the early 1946, Gus organized a ski jumping training camp in Lillehammer and had the top ski jumpers in Norway at this camp including Georg Thrane, Thorleif Schjelderup, Ragnar Baklid, Olav Odden, Claus Dahl, Odd Winquist, Frank Waastad Olsen, Torbjorn Falkanger, Christian Mohn, Sigurd Olsen, Arne Hoel, and Hugo Persson. Gus had only one hill record in Norway and that was 63 meters in Rindalsbakken, south of Lillehammer on the west side of Mjosa.

In the fall of 1945 and early 1946, Gus lived in Oslo where he continued his education. Gus studied at Oslo Handelsgym, which provided the highest level of commercial education available in Norway. He completed an advanced business degree in one year. Gus stayed with his cousin Harald Thorsen on the 3rd floor in Tidemandsgt. 27, a home owned by his Uncle Christian Fredrik Christensen, who lived on the second floor.

Even though Gus had a busy life, pursuing his studies, he never stopped competing. In fact, every Sunday he would be ski jumping. He continued to place high in most of the meets and won several of them, but he was about to become a national hero. This was the day that

Gus's 2nd jump at the 1946 Holmenkollen.

changed the course of his life forever. In his own words, he described that day:

> The biggest, by far, was winning the junior class at Holmenkollen in Oslo in 1946, the first competition in Holmenkollen since the end of the war. The huge crowd of 106,000 spectators made this a real national holiday and the competition was listened to over the radio by almost everybody in Norway. The special jumping competition was divided in two classes, those under 20 years and those over. This competition was at that time considered the World Series of Ski Jumping, so overnight my name was known by everyone in Norway who listened to the competition. Each region in Norway got a quota for the number of jumpers, which they could send to compete in Holmenkollen. Our region had a quota of 4 jumpers, and I was lucky to be one of them, together with my two good friends Odd Winquist and Frank Waastad Olsen (all 3 were juniors) and Harald Mathisen. Every ski jumper's dream was to be able to compete in Holmenkollen and specially to win one of the familiar silver trophies was even more exciting. I jumped 61 meters and 62 meters, but had excellent form points (second best of all the 250 jumpers who competed that day) and ended up winning, so my name suddenly came into the lime light and in the press. That great day changed my life, since the result and subsequent performance put me on the Norwegian Ski Jumping Team.

Among those thousands watching this momentous post-war event was the Norwegian Royal family. In the USA, as a member of the University of Washington ski team, Gus would go on to become a NCAA National Ski Champion.

Holmenkollen Ski Jump, 1946

Chapter 9
Cruising Into The Future

Before Gus got his chance to tour the United States with the Norwegian Ski Jumping Team, his father had gotten him a job as an assistant purser in the summer of 1946. The Norwegian passenger liner was called "Stavangerfjord." According to Gus, the ship weighed almost 16,000 thousand tons and carried about 700 passengers. As luck would have it, the purser, Arne Blix, who was a friend of his father, had an opening for one trip because one of the assistant pursers was going to take a vacation. Even though he was a lowly employee, Gus was clearly proud of his new position. "I got a nice white uniform which had a very thin golden stripe on the shoulder pad. I was, I think, the lowest officer on board this ship. My job was to work in the office on the ship, and in the evening we were to introduce passengers around and to entertain them and make them feel at home."

Stavangerfjord sailed between Oslo and New York City with stops in Stavanger and Bergen before it headed across the Atlantic. While sailing along the Norwegian coast and before they got to Bergen, the pursers worked diligently to make up all the passenger lists with all information on the passengers, i.e. who was in each cabin, where they were going, how many suitcases they had, their ages and other personal information. As the behemoth ship crossed the Atlantic there were office hours to serve the passengers, to make change, cash travelers checks, give other passenger information, provide safe deposit boxes etc. Gus was delighted to have his own private cabin on the main deck close to the office. He and his fellow workers ate in the main dining room with the passengers.

Gus was one of four assistant pursers who were single men. So it was no surprise that they would take turns perusing the gang plank as passengers were coming aboard, to see what kind of young ladies were coming aboard as passengers, "Which would make the crossing more pleasant."

The crossing took about 14 days, so the crew had plenty of time to get acquainted with many of the passengers. Navigating the Atlantic meant some heavy seas, and sometimes just a few of the 700 passengers would show up in the dining room, the rest were down below in their cabins sicker than dogs. The high seas were full of adventure, and, yes, romance. "After a few days at sea some of the ladies got very romantic, so we had to watch our steps. We had some nice private parties down in the hospital section of the ship, a good spot for this since few people got sick and the first aid area was seldom used."

Gus was filled with awe when the ship arrived in New York Harbor. What a moment for a young man on the cusp of a whole new life. Like so many immigrants before him, Gus was enthralled by the iconic welcome of a lovely lady. "I ran up to the bridge of the ship to watch as we passed the Statue of Liberty, but the Captain asked me what I was doing on the bridge, then proceeded to tell me to get back to my job." (Little did Gus know that someday he would be an American citizen.)

After unloading all passengers, luggage and freight and finishing our work in the office, the crew had got some time off before they headed back out in only three days. With half of their monthly pay in cash, they headed uptown for sightseeing and shopping. In the summer of '46, Manhattan was hopping; the war over, the troops were home, and the air was thick with optimism and music. "We went to Jack Dempsey's bar on Broadway, and we went to the Cotton Club and listened to Cab Calloway and his orchestra. And we went to the Rockefeller Center, and watched the Rockettes dance in line in the big theater there which could hold some 6,000 people, same as the whole population of Lillehammer at that time."

Gus was sure he'd never get back to New York City, so he bought a lot of gifts to take back home. He was enthralled with the skyscrapers. As many tourists still do today, the Norwegian boys had challenges using public transportation. "We used the subway system and elevated trains several times, but we ended up getting on the wrong train and crossed over the river into Brooklyn. We could see our ship at the Pier on South Manhattan as we went further and further away. We tried to talk to a conductor, but his Brooklyn English was impossible to understand. We finally found a passenger who could help direct us to the right train so we could get back to our ship."

Gus was lucky not to be among a few crew members who tried to smuggle contraband on to the ship. Many years later, he had fond memories of shipboard shenanigans:

> I can remember a few of our crew members came late back to the ship, they had bought a case of whiskey to take back to Norway. But the gangplank had already been pulled, so some crew members on board lowered a boom with rope to the crew on the dock. They tied the case of whiskey to the rope, and as they swung over towards the ship the case hit the side of the ship and broke most of the bottles. The men climbed aboard up the rope. But this did not go unnoticed by the Captain who was on the bridge as the ship was leaving the dock. The crew members involved were grounded and were fired when the ship returned to Norway.

The crew didn't make much money, so it didn't take long to spend half month's pay. Reflecting on still perilous times, though, they received extra pay called mine pay, because of the risk of all the mines that the Germans had laid all over the oceans.

When Gus got back to Oslo another assistant purser wanted to take a vacation, so he eagerly agreed to take another trip to New York. As with everything in his life, Gus fully embraced and made the best of his job.

> The trip back to Norway was a lot of fun, because I got more chances to practice my English and people who were heading for Norway were anxious about their arrival in Norway and wanted to know how it was in Norway during the war and occupation. This crossing was done in the fall, so the weather in the Atlantic would be pretty rough. We had fun on board after the first few days of office work was done. We introduced people around, and danced with some of the passengers.

Gus developed a love for the sea that would last a lifetime. "I really enjoyed being at sea and could have easily chosen that as a job in the future." But in the fall of 1946, Gus secured a position as a sales clerk in Sigmund Ruud's sporting goods store in Oslo on Kirkeveien near Majorstua. Gus's life revolved around skiing even at work "I worked together with Asbjorn Ruud, the youngest brother of Sigmund Ruud, they had both been World ski jumping champions, and Asbjorn Ruud won the over 20 class in Holmenkollen in 1946 when I won the under 20 class."

Gus's command of English would also prove to be a great asset at the store.

> I had always hoped to go to USA to study at a university, so I appreciated the experience I got at Sigmund Ruud's store. I worked there over 2 months. In a letter which I wrote home dated Nov. 4, 1946, I wrote about an interesting experience when an English business man representing the sport firm Caxton from India came into the store, and Sigmund Ruud had left on a business trip to Sweden, and office manager, Oyvind Ruud, did not feel too comfortable in the English language, so he asked me to kind of take care of this man. I took him out on the town, had dinner with him, showed him around town, and I took him to the barbershop so he could get cleaned up. We had dinner at Frognerseter up near Holmenkollen and all was paid for by the firm. I talked English like mad, and the customer was happy about that. I showed him the view from that area. After we got back to the store in about 2 hours I talked to him about how to handle the business transaction.

Because business became slow and had to be reorganized, Sigmund Ruud had to cut back. Gus graciously volunteered to leave the store and traveled back home to Lillehammer after what he viewed as "A very nice experience at the store in Oslo." That was Gus's attitude toward his life…he seemed to always focus on the *good*. From that point on, the goal was to get accepted to a college in the USA.

Gus contacted the Scandinavian- American Foundation and other organizations to get some support. Once again, his contacts helped him in his education and in his sport. "Einar Bergsland and Sigmund Ruud from Oslo were involved in selecting a Norwegian ski jumping team to tour the USA at the invitation of the U.S. Ski Association. Because of my first place in Holmenkollen in 1946 they recommended that I be part of the group to travel to USA. Others were Arnold Kongsgaard, Ragnar Baklid, Harald Hauge, and Odd Harsheim."

In February of 1947, Gus left Norway on the Stavangerfjord, but this time, not as an employee of the ship. This time, Gus Raaum was beginning a trip of a lifetime, and a whole new beginning.

The Norwegian passenger liner, Stavangerfjord.

Part II

The American Letters 1947-1951

The following chapters are extracted from letters Gus Raaum wrote home to his parents. In another time and place, letters were the thread that tethered families, friends and lovers. The art of writing letters is almost extinct. Thankfully, these were preserved for the Raaum family history.

"When I traveled to the United States in February, 1947 as part of the Norwegian Ski Jumping Team, I had no idea what the future held for me. When we left Oslo on the S/S Stavangerfjord bound for New York I was sure the trip would only last about one month, then I would return to Lillehammer, and pursue my education in business. Thanks to placing first in Holmenkollen in junior class in 1946, and based on recommendations by Einar Bergsland and Sigmund Ruud, I was included on this Norwegian Ski Jumping Team. The United States Ski Association had invited this team to

tour the United States to take part in competitions and exhibitions. This was the first such tour after World War II, and people all over the United Sates who had family and friends in Norway were eager to meet us. Since I expected to be asked to speak about my trip when I returned home, I asked my mother to save the letters I wrote home, so I did not have to keep notes. She did. In fact, she saved them for 4 ½ years. I translated these letters to English so my children and grandchildren might enjoy reading about my experiences during my early years in the United States."

Gustav Raaum

Chapter 10
Shipping Out To Sea & Ski

Stavangerfjord, Feb. 13, 1947

Gus and his teammates left Norway on the Stavangerfjord and arrived in New York City on Feb. 14th, 1947. Gus was one day away from reaching New York when he wrote, "The weather has been great except yesterday and today when the ship has plunged half way in the ocean on every wave, but I have not had any sign of seasickness." Gus had already earned his sea legs with having taken two trips back and forth across the Atlantic as an assistant purser. Gus already knew his

Gus (far left) with teammates aboard Stavangerfjord, 1947.

father's friend, Arne Blix, a ship purser; therefore, they had permission to have the run of the ship. Naturally, they spent a lot of time in first class.

The boys kept themselves fit by running, gymnastics, deck tennis and ping pong. Of course, they spent a lot of time on deck waxing their beloved skis. During this trip Gustav and his teammates were treated like celebrities by curious passengers and were constantly being photographed. They were regulars in the Captain's cabin for tea, and were also offered drinks. "But we would stick to beer and soft drinks with the upcoming competitions in mind." The young men were also invited to some dances, but were required to be in bed by midnight because they had to be up by 8 a.m.

Once the team arrived in New York, they were taken to the Waldorf Astoria for a banquet. Even though the team only spent eight hours in N.Y., this stylish welcome was the beginning of a great adventure. From there, they headed to Brattleboro, Vermont where Gus made a short, but well-received speech.

After Brattleboro, the team boarded a train and headed west. On the way, they passed Niagara Falls on their journey to Chicago where they only stayed a few hours. Gus enjoyed the train "…which had a nice club car, large smoking cars and restaurant cars." The team arrived in Ishpeming, MI where the US National Championships were to take place. They slept in a fire station the first night. Although Gus was disgruntled with the organizers about the sleeping arrangements, he found Ishpeming to be "a very cozy small town of about 9-10,000 inhabitants, lots of snow, beautiful weather and really nice people."

Like the other teammates, Gus was somewhat anxious about going down Suicide Hill. He said, "The in-run is scaffold which is the steepest and most scary I have seen." He wrenched his left ankle a little bit at his first attempt to go down the hill, but fared better than the American skier who broke his ankle.

There was a fabulous reception in the Norwegian Club in Brooklyn, MI. There were speeches and a lot of picture taking. The teams traveled back to the east coast and delivered their skis to Grand Central Station. Once again, there was a lavish reception at the Norwegian Club in Manhattan where the men were treated as celebrities; swamped by photographers. All this attention brought lots of female admirers, too. Unfortunately, training came first. Much to the girls' chagrin, the boys needed to be in bed (alone) by 11 p.m.

From there, the team traveled by night train and awakened in Brattleboro. Gus competed, but had several "unlucky" runs and sprained his ankle. While he was there, they all got to meet Merrill Mezzy Barber, "America's next best ski jumper." Gus says, Mezzy Barber "…who beat us in Brattleboro, is going on to Holmenkollen."

This time was a whirlwind filled with banquets and award ceremonies, and even had Gus doing a radio interview. Thank goodness his English skills were improving by the hour!

Gus and his team went on to Iron Mountain, located approximately 11 miles from Ishpeming, Michigan. Although his ankle had improved, there was bad weather. Gustav wrote, "The tournament is being postponed 6 times due to wind and heavy snow fall."

Along with his teammates he met the governor of Michigan, Kim Sigler, who made the mistake of asking the team how everything was in Gothenburg (Goteborg, Sweden). "We were surprised and lost respect for him," Gus said. He noted that the governor was treated like a king with everyone standing whenever he entered a room.

Here, too, the team is treated like royalty; mobbed by journalist, photographers, and autograph seekers when they get to their ski jumping hill. "People are nuts," Gus says, "…we had to write our name on collars, on ski shirts, on dollar bills, on table clothes, etc." He's also amazed by thousands of cars at the venue. But Gus's ankle was still very swollen and stiff but he was able to complete five jumps skiing straight forward until he stopped because he could not turn the skis. Bad weather continued to lead to postponement of competition events on the Monday, Feb. 24th, his parent's 24th wedding anniversary.

Being the good son he was, Gustav congratulated them amidst his numerous social activities interspersed with some ski jumps.

On Friday, Feb. 28th, a competition was held at Suicide Hill. Gustav was still unable to jump well due to his weak ankle. He came in 8th place and was awarded a small sugar and cream set. The next day's competition was at Iron Mountain where Gustav complained "They have no idea about preparing a landing hill here, they look like sledding hills of ice."

In March, the team traveled by train to Chicago in first class with excellent adjustable seats, smoking cars with soft reclining chairs, and a nice bar. Gus's impressions of Chicago were not positive. "Oh my how dirty this town is, I would not want to live in this town for anything in the world." From Chicago they traveled by plane to Salt Lake. Gus described Salt Lake City as, "Beautiful with many beautiful buildings." While there they did much socializing and finally had a gorgeous day. "The hill was in excellent shape, "Gustav said, "They ski packed it often, and it was the first time we have experienced in America a completely successful and well organized competition done by Utah Ski Club in Salt Lake City." For placing 2nd in the longest jump Gustav received a trophy with a skier on top, he described "like his Torleif Haug statue" gold plated in a goldsmith store and an adjustable pencil. He had thoughts about buying a gold watch with his winnings.

Throughout this time, Gus met many young women. One of them sent him a letter, saying she had taken a picture of him "on the hill." She wanted Gus to write to her because "He was her ideal." Understandably, Gus had no idea who this girl was. "I am sure there were over 100 girls who took pictures there, so I can't remember her, but that is America."

Challenger Inn, Sun Valley, ID, March 1947

Today it's called "The Sun Valley Inn", but back in 1947, it was called "The Challenger Inn." Gus loved Sun Valley, Idaho and called it a "fantastic ski resort." And, of course it was also home to the rich and famous. Ernest Hemingway brought it to public attention in the late 1930's. Gus and the gang enjoyed two heated outdoor pools where they could, "Take off your skis and put on your swimsuit and go swimming in the open air."

For the first time, the whole team was together, including the slalom skiers. At breakfast they met many world famous slalom and downhill skiers from Switzerland, Austria, France and from the USA. "In addition," Gus said, "There are many film stars here and an impressive number of cute girls. Oy, oy!! So far I have only met one of them. Her name is Ruth."

There was a big slalom competition with all the top skiers, namely Canada's best lady twins, Wurtele, Pfeifer, Ronninger, Matt, Molitor, McLean, Prager and Gordon Wren. They were the top alpine skiers in the world. Gus seemed entranced when he described the place:

"The terrain is fantastic, and chair lifts go up and up in all directions, and there are great runs, so we can really go downhill. There was not a cloud in the sky, and we are all walking around looking like cooked lobsters in our faces, and it is burning."

Gus describes alpine skiing on Baldy Mountain, "It had beautiful runs with a drop of some 900 meters." He also rubbed shoulders with the super stars of sports history. On one of these ski outings he jumped with Gordon Wren. Gordon Wren was the only American to qualify for four Olympic skiing events. In 1948 at the Winter Games in St. Moritz, Switzerland, Wren placed second in combined jumping and fifth in special jumping. He was also the first American ski jumper to break the 300-foot mark. Gustav notes that he is a super guy both sports wise and personally. He considered him the world's best skier. "He races slalom like a God," Gustav says, "and downhill likewise, and on top of that he jumps just as well as us in smaller hills, a super guy who I take my hat off for, likewise for Alf Engen, he is now 39 years old and he is next best in slalom and downhill and a very good jumper." Engen was a Norwegian-American skier who set several ski jumping world records during the 1930's, and helped establish numerous ski resorts in the western United States. He was also known as the "pioneer of powder skiing."

Gustav attended so many fantastic banquets. On this trip, there were nicely decorated tables, stylish people, good food, speeches, and behavior etc. and awarding of prizes and the Harriman Cup. Gus was very admiring of the women skiers. "When you see these fantastic downhill and slalom skiers (ladies) in evening gowns, they look so elegant, cute and classy, one can't understand that they are flying down the mountain at 90 KM/hour with their life hanging in a thread."

One of the highlights of that evening was dancing with Paula Kann, the best US lady alpine skier. During the final dance of the evening they danced cheek to cheek. "She was very cute and charming," Gus said, "…and she is on the Olympic Team and hoping for a trip to Norway." He didn't have the courage to invite her for a moonlight stroll as she sat at the table with Tony Matt, America's best alpine skier. It was a wonderful evening he would never forget.

The last day Gustav was in Sun Valley he was with Pierre Jalbert, the Canadian slalom and downhill champion, and Ruth-Marie Stewart, who finished 2nd in downhill. Before the team left Sun Valley, they also met Norma Shearer, a famous Hollywood actress. According to Gus, "She expressed her excitement about our ski jumping, and especially my form." At the time, the wealthy actress was married to a Sun Valley ski teacher. Ski stars and movie stars were a few of many celebrities Gus would encounter throughout this grand adventure.

After their Sun Valley stay they traveled approximately 5 hours by bus to Boise. There, they were having the competition for the main selection of the US team for the 1948 Olympics. Gustav said that he talked to a phenomenal skier by the name of Andrea Mead who was only 14 years old and won the slalom race and finished second in combined among the world's elite in the trials for the Olympic team. As an American alpine ski racer, Mead eventually competed in three Winter Olympics, and was the first to win two Olympic gold medals.

Now, it was on to Seattle. Gus had little idea that someday he would call the Emerald City home.

Gus (4th from left) & teammates arrive in Seattle, 1947.

Chapter 11
The Bluest Skies In Seattle

The ski team traveled from Sun Valley to Boise by bus. The five hour trip was comfortable since Gus said it had no similarity to Norwegian buses. "We slept most of the way in soft, wide chairs which we could adjust almost to a horizontal position." They flew out of Boise, with a quick stop in Portland, and arrived in Seattle four hours later.

Gus described Seattle "As being a nice city of about 600,000 inhabitants." The hotel the team stayed in was the Olympic Hotel, one of the city's finest. Gus recalled it as "being spectacular and the biggest hotel in Seattle with 2,000 beds." This was in March of 1947, and because Gus was used to long winters and cool Norwegian springs, he was amazed by beans growing and flowers blooming.

The day after the team got to Seattle, they traveled up to the jumping hill which was as far from Seattle as Gus thought Kongsberg was from Oslo. "There was lots of snow but it was rotten so they went in deep when they landed, so the captain refused to let us jump." The team found out that they would not have permission to start in the competition either Saturday or Sunday in the Olympic try-outs. They were all very upset because they came to America to compete against

American jumpers, and when they had a chance to meet them all in the same place they were not allowed to start.

Gus had a lot of fun during this trip: banquets, interviews with the press and lots of nice girls. One big highlight was going to a drive-in movie for the first time in his life. "We sat in the car the whole time watching the movie. We saw the movie through the front windshield, and the sound came through a small loudspeaker which they hang on the window of each car." After that, they went to a drive-in café. "You park the car outside the restaurant then a cute waitress comes running to your car before you get your motor turned off." For Gus, this was a big slice of American life. "We have been to a movie and to a restaurant and not even gotten out of our car."

It turned out that Seattle would be a huge turning point in Gus's life. Originally, he was delayed because his fellow teammate, Harald Hauge, was hospitalized for an illness. Gus had planned to travel to the eastern United States for a year and then head home. But he met a group of men whom he referred to as "Big Shots" who convinced him to apply to the University of Washington. While they were having dinner at an exclusive restaurant Gus called The Tennis Club, they offered to help him find a job salmon fishing in Alaska to cover tuition. Remarkably, Gus passed the admission test on the first try. At the time, UW had about 15,000 students. To Gus's delight, 6,000 were girls. He started with Business and Economics. What a challenge it must have been for this young man having to learn so much so quickly. "Think about yourself coming into a lecture where there is a professor who stands there and talks and talks so fast and using so many words that are foreign to me." Gus would stay up studying all night to catch up and at the same time finish daily assignments. He would credit his bookkeeping and geography courses at the commercial college in Oslo for helping him pass. The hope was that he could be classified as a junior since he had some college education while in Norway.

During this time, Gus lived with, "The wonderful and kind Olav Ulland from Kongsberg. He started with 5 cents and now owns a large, well known sporting goods store here in Seattle. He has been the best ski jumper here in the West since he arrived." As part of the Seattle Ski Club, Gus got to know Olav very well because he was also his coach. The members enjoyed a cabin on Snoqualmie Pass where they could sleep over, and train on jumping hills at Beaver Lake Hill, and the Milwaukee Bowl which was considered a major ski area, comparable, but not as luxurious as Sun Valley. The Milwaukee Bowl held a Class-A ski jump that was built in 1941, and was known as the largest ski jump in North America at that time. Many national championship events were held there including the 1948 Olympics jumping team tryouts. Unfortunately, on December 2nd, 1949 the lodge burned down but the ski area continued to operate out of train cars until 1951.

Originally, Olav Ulland came to the United States to coach Seattle Ski Club jumpers. One sports writer said, "Ski jumping was just in his blood. That was his life." Once he was in the Northwest, he decided to stay. Ulland was an Olympic coach and judge whose store in Seattle was known for its "sniagrab" (bargains spelled backwards) pre-ski equipment sales. He never forgot his Norwegian roots; his home was always open to Norwegians going through the immigration process. (Olav Ulland died in 2003 at the ripe old age of 92.)

In the spring of 1947, Gus moved out of Ulland's home and into the Sigma Nu fraternity house. Located only minutes from the university, more than 50 American students lived there. (There was one other Norwegian ski jumper besides Gus.) Gus told his parents, "I am learning to speak English, and all the boys are very helpful when I do not understand something." (Another milestone, Gus learned how to drive.) The fraternity house gave him a sense of belonging.

> The whole group is like a family. We have a big
> living room with sofas and arm chairs, fire place
> and grand piano and two other big rooms where we
> mostly play bridge. There is also a very nice
> veranda where we can sun tan.

The rest of the house was amazing, offering a gymnasium, dining hall and library. Parties and dances were all part of college life, but study and good grades were the top priority. Most of all, Gus found the fellowship he so desperately needed being so far from his home and country.

The diversity of the campus also intrigued Gus, "There are students from 27 different countries," he said. "At a nice international get together a few days ago I was there with students from India, Iran, England, Turkey, Palestine, Peru, China, Argentina, Philippines, Chile, Greece, Russia, Panama, Bolivia, Korea, very interesting."

During this time, an interesting job offer came up that he shared with his parents and wanted to hear his dad's opinion regarding it. George Jensen, the gentlemen offering him the job, had a large export and import firm dealing with foreign countries. He was acting as buying agent for large department stores, and arranged exports for large companies of all kinds of goods to all countries. He told Gus if he wanted to he could come down to his office and start his own new department. Gus wrote to his father:

> He would fix me up with a desk, telephone etc. I could establish contact with firms in Norway which would be interested in exporting goods to the USA, and his firm here would pay all telephone, postage etc. and arrange for the purchase of the goods, and I would take care of the correspondence and received 35% of the profits.

Gus thought it was a generous offer that would allow him to get a lot of trade and business experience in addition to his studies. He would have spent his Saturdays doing this job as nothing was going on at the university then. In the end, Gus decided against it because of not having a work permit and it would take too much time.

Trouble with the language in his English Speech class and in his geography class continued to be a challenge at the beginning, especially topics such as atomic energy. It's hard to imagine how difficult this would be for an immigrant, but Gus muscled through, hitting the books into the night and over the weekends. He was determined to make the most of this opportunity. And speaking of opportunity, Gus was asked to do his own presentation in his geography class about Norway. He did an hour presentation "…about mountains, the climate, the precipitation, vegetation, farming, forest industry, all industries, fishing etc." Clearly, Gus was in his comfort zone. "I specially mentioned Lillehammer as a big tourist center with excellent ski terrain, hotels, about airplane connections with Denmark."

For Gus, this time is filled with pride and some anxiety especially around money. In some of his correspondences with his folks, he is hesitant about asking for help, but it's clear he needs it. He writes, "If they should by chance get ahold of a few dollars, that he would not refuse them." He was also stretching his independence at the same time when he wrote: "Mamma does not have to be anxious for her youngest son; he'll make it, even outside his mother's skirt!!" This definitely sounds like something a typical twenty-one year old man would say.

In June of 1947, Gus profusely thanked his parents for the $10 they'd sent. They were relieved to hear that he'd turned down the job offer with the export company. Gus knew in his heart that his education had to come first. He had applied for a scholarship for his next year of college but hadn't heard anything yet. He explained to his parents what a tight budget he's on and where his money goes, but feels he'll make it one way or another. Thankfully, he has so many friends willing to loan him money if need be. One day, he would look back on his days as an impoverished student, knowing he was truly a self-made man.

Final exams were keeping him very busy, he wrote:

I have taken one exam, English speech. When I only had two days to study, so I really had to cram and pick my way through 9 books to learn about use of voice, phrases, pauses, listening, preparation of a speech etc. To my great surprise I answered all the questions more or less complete, of course, and we got only 35 minutes to answer the questions. I had a conference with my teacher in speech several days ago, and he bragged terribly about me.

Once again, Gus's hard work paid off. The teacher told him that he did beautifully and would be given a B. "I almost made a backwards somersault with a twist," Gustav said, "because I almost thought I had flunked the whole thing." This teacher seldom gave A's so Gustav couldn't help but be pleased and proud of himself. He goes on to tell his parents how successful he was after giving a 10 minute speech about what made the German invasion of Norway easy. Many students and the speech teacher complimented him afterwards. "Apparently I must have done this perfectly," he related. "They expressed great excitement over how much better English I speak now compared to when I started."

As he progressed in his studies, he decided to change from a Business Administration major to an Accounting major. He felt that the professor teaching accounting is one of the best he could have while the professor who is not so good will be teaching B.A. In addition, Gus believed the accounting teacher "…can speak English so a regular poor guy like me can understand what he says." Another reason is the reputation of the Accounting Department which is considered one of the best in the USA. For Gus, his studies were an uphill climb. "Here in America you have to cross every T otherwise they think it is an L. I was not aware of that until two days ago, so the poor professors who have to correct papers will have a hard time with my papers." Another bit of good news was he was able to get a Social

Security number without showing any work permit which he'd not yet received.

After taking his final exams, Gus left for Alaska by plane on June 15th. He would be heading to the coastal town of Ketchikan, then take a small plane to Waterfall where the Union Bay Cannery was located. Once again, his good friend, Olav Ulland loaned him a lot of equipment and clothing for his trip. (Ulland knew what to bring because he had been stationed in Alaska during the war.) He needed to join the Alaska Fishermen's Union before taking the cannery job; otherwise the owner of the canneries might risk a strike from the other workers. Even though he was just starting his Alaska adventure, his hopes were already focused on training for the ski jumping National Championships. Two or three of his friends had been thinking about traveling to Sun Valley for a week during Christmas to train. As a sign of the time, Gus had been smoking throughout his athletic challenges, but he finally makes a decision to stop smoking, one he'd made in the fall of 1946. "Oddly enough I have tried a cigarette a few times but it did not taste good at all, so I am done with that." What he wasn't enjoying either was American food. He confided in his parents, "I can tell you that I can't stand the food here. I would love to have a Norwegian breakfast." Either way, he was eating the breakfast of champions!

Chapter 12
North To Alaska (June 1947)

With a suitcase and a backpack, Gus arrived at the airport at 7:30 a.m. ready for this next adventure to Alaska. But, alas, the passenger count was incorrect, and he and ten others were left behind. He tried "…to move heaven and earth" to no avail, and had to wait until the next day to take off. (Fortunately, the airline paid for a hotel room.) The Clipper plane held 42 passengers and provided a meal. Gus recalled, "After 3 ½ hours of, mostly fog, we landed on a large airfield near Ketchikan in Alaska." (Ketchikan reminded Gus of Brevik.) The next leg took Gus to a lake where a small seaplane awaited him. Gus sat right next to the pilot for the short trip. When they landed, fog had set in. After a short delay, he boarded a third plane and headed for Waterfall, a small fishing village with 10-20 houses. Waterfall Cannery was built in 1912 as a salmon processing facility. When Gus arrived it was still the Wild West. "There are some Indians here, and only a few yards behind the houses big bears!! I have not seen any yet, but it is not going to take long according to the group here."

The topography brought back memories of his homeland; islands and water and lots of trees. Scattered among the landscape were totem poles. But there wouldn't be a lot of time for sightseeing once work started. The day began at 7:15 a.m. with breakfast and continued (with food breaks) until 5:30 p.m. Thank goodness, the food was as good as the scenery. "The food is fantastic, reminds me of almost a fine Norwegian hotel. We get as many oranges as we want. On Sundays we get beer at dinner."

His dorm room housed twelve men and four of them were Norwegian. The men had one nail to hang belongings on, and a "wooden butter crate" for the rest. Also, no radios. Because they all lived together, they often got sick together, too. This was not a place for the faint of heart. "Here you can't call your mama either to get some cough medicine, warm milk or food. If we get sick, then we get sick."

The work consisted of making salmon traps out of 160' of chicken wire. The heavy lifting was keeping Gus in shape, "...after pushing a pencil for so long." Eventually two men would be sent out on a "log flat" with a trap. They lived in a small shack during that time, which reminded Gus of "...a pig house where you barely have room for two beds." The log flats were slippery and dangerous; one wrong step on rough waters meant a fall into the ocean. (Hyperthermia could overtake a man in less than an hour.) The waves would hit the side of the cabin walls. There was no electricity, and limited drinking/ bathing water. The times were tough out in the middle of nowhere. "We have to cook our own food, watch the traps against fish thieves, so we have a rifle to shoot against approaching problems." Luckily,

Gus was taught how to shoot at an early age by his father. Gus took along school books because there was plenty of time to study.

The bears were never far away. In fact, they would see them several times a day. The closest Gus came was 50 meters (about 160 feet). Close enough, especially when Gus saw a mother and her two cubs. "They are cute, but the mother is very dangerous when they have cubs." Speaking of dangerous, booze and bar fights were also part of the Alaskan life. Gus and his buddies celebrated July 4th by traveling an hour and a half by boat to a liquor store. "Most of the guys got drunk, got into bar fights with the Indians, lost money, ruined their clothes etc., knives were even drawn!! Gus was able to "take it easy" and avoid the melee.

The only connection to Ketchikan was by plane. The men would run to the plane looking for mail, and possibly some "white girls." Gus explained why they were not allowed to become involved with native women. "If you get discovered with an Indian girl here, you have to marry her and live here for 7 years, and then you can get a divorce and travel to where you want. Not a happy circumstance." It's obvious, Gus's courting days would have to resume when he returned to Seattle.

In a letter from Alaska, he did confide in his parents, though, that "American girls think of nothing else except marriage. They can hardly cook potatoes or sew, just want to have fun." Gus had no idea that the perfect American girl would one day be his wife!

The summer in Alaska proved to be a big adventure, and a test of skills and endurance. Gus passed with flying colors. He learned to live in tight quarters with a co-worker, work tirelessly in all kinds of weather; deal with armed thieves who would descend in the dead of night to steal their catch. Even small things like hygiene were a challenge. He could only wash himself and his clothes after a big rain when clean water was plentiful. He continued to write home, always beginning his letters with, "Thousand thanks for your letters." His mother was in a constant state of worry, but he would assure her, "Stay cool mama, I am neither dead or eaten by sharks, have not broken any arms or legs, teeth and my eyes are okay." He continued. "Mama put all your worry up in the attic---behind the cookie tins."

Through it all, Gus maintained an attitude that would sustain him for his entire life. He said, "I'll be happy wherever I am if I have a good job, and like it, and have a good time, and live happily." For Gus, the best was yet to come.

Gus tending a fish trap in Ketchikan - 1947

Chapter 13
Sun Valley And Beyond

The college year of 1947 to 1948 brought a much needed scholarship from the university. Gus was definitely an indigent student. "The greatest need is probably shoes," he wrote to his parents. "My stockings are full of holes." The job in Alaska had left him in good shape, but overweight. He started to train vigorously: running, gymnastics, swimming, diving, and water polo. Gus quickly lost the extra pounds and was ready for an excellent ski season. "I am going to represent the University of Washington in Sun Valley in the National Collegiate Ski Championships." He was also getting excellent grades. Life was looking good, and Gus described it as "wonderland." In the female department things were also going well. "There has been plenty of girls, now I can choose between 4 of them if we go out." The fraternity house threw lots of dances, too. On one occasion, Gus was asked to paint the wall of the gym. "I painted clouds, stars, stormy ocean, fish etc. on three walls, which made everybody happy. I did not realize I had artistic blood in me." Gus had no trouble meeting girls on the competition road. This encounter was in Salt Lake City at a dance:

> After 2 hours she was excited about me. After 4 hours, she was very much in love with me. I asked her to send me a picture of her, and I have received a large fine

picture which is located here on my desk together with a picture of Mamma and Papa and Dick as well.

December of '47 was an exciting time. Gus told his parents, "Believe it or not, I took part in two cross-country tryouts for our team and among 25 skiers I finished 2nd in both races. The result is that I have been selected to represent UW both in cross-country and jumping in the US National collegiate Championships in Sun Valley." And since it was December, Christmas and thoughts of home were on his mind. "The house is beautifully decorated for the Christmas holidays, and the streets in the university district are decorated almost like they are in Lillehammer with evergreen branches hanging over the street with all kinds of colored lights." Gus and his team made their way to Sun Valley but were met with the absence of snow, so they had to travel farther out to find it. Eventually they did, but on the way, Gus lost one of his slalom skies, and could only train in cross-country. While out skiing on an alpine course, he had a close encounter with a celebrity that almost ended in disaster.

I almost crashed into Mrs. Gary Cooper!! She had fallen and was laying in the most narrow part of the course when I was coming down a steep hill at full speed. The only thing I could do was to take a chance at passing between two trees which were only 2 feet apart. I almost closed my eyes and speeded through and barely made it, but broke out in a cold sweat. (women!!)

Other celebrity encounters were much more pleasant. At a Christmas party dance, Gus spotted Ingrid Bergman, her husband, Mr. & Mrs. Gary Cooper (regulars at Sun Valley) and Henry Ford and his family. At the lodge's sports store, Gus even chatted with Gary Cooper and got a glimpse of Claudette Colbert. At Sun Valley, Gus certainly had a window on the rich and the famous. This trip would also prove to be a tremendous success for Gus. He became the U.S. NCAA jumping champion. "I ended up the day's hero and beat the next man by almost 13 points."

At the celebration banquet Gus was described this way by the man giving him the honor:

The first prize to the man who is a little new to us, but we will see more of him in the future. The charming and always smiling Gustav Raaum of the University of Washington." (Tor Arneberg, Christian Bugge and Gus were also elected honorary members of Sun Valley Ski Club) The announcer described all of them as, "Nice Norwegians who displayed good skiing and spirit.

From there on out, it was a whirlwind of activity. After Sun Valley, Gus took part in competitions every weekend. He traveled with the UW team to Canada and received the royal treatment. "We were treated like kings, lived and ate privately. The whole place reminded me of Lillehammer." When the jumping concluded, Gus was introduced as, "a fabulous jumper, one of the best in the world". He proved them right. "I won way ahead of the next man, the largest margin I've ever had in competition." He attracted the attention of the media being interviewed on radio and filmed for a news reel.

But the glamour ended when Gus got back to school and the challenge to survive classes and the cost of living. He had to work in the kitchen; washing dishes and peeling potatoes. He received free room and board in exchange. Gus described his financial situation this way. "My check book starts to look like a thin thread." His parents were only able to send a minimal amount of money. It was a constant struggle to keep up his grades, work in the kitchen and continue to devote himself to his athletic goals. But he didn't give up, even if it meant burning the midnight oil bent over his books until four in the morning

The competitions continued, with many trophies and some disappointments. After a less than stellar performance at the Northern Division of Collegiate Championships, Gus wrote to his parents, "I am well known as a style jumper in this country, so that must be the reason for this. Enough about that, it was my darkest day this winter. I jumped like a box of wood that had been tipped over." On top of that,

L-R: Ole Lie, Olav Ulland, Gunnar Sunde and Gus

he was a month behind in his studies. Even though Gus practically lived on coffee, he still pulled a B average.

On one of Gus's many trips to Sun Valley, he was invited by 20th Century Fox to jump in some scenes in a film. He was at his best. The film was called "That Wonderful Urge" starring Gene Tierney and Tyrone Power. No big movie deal came out of it, however, Gus loved the whole experience, and was told that he performed the best out of all the jumpers. Many months later, when the movie was released, Gus went to see it in a theater. Unfortunately, to his great disappointment, all his scenes were cut. That's showbiz!

That year, Gus summarized his winter competition this way, "I took 6 first places, 3 second places and one 6th." But the struggles of being a poor college student were always present. In one letter he tells his parents he's been wearing the same suit for about three years. Also, he needs dental work. "They charge minimum $10 per cavity, and since it is over 1 ½ [years] since last time, I am afraid I'll have at least 4 cavities." Judging from today's dental cost, it might seem a pittance, but for Gus, it was a fortune. At that time, his fortune was in medals. That would have to be enough to help him forge ahead…and that he did.

Chapter 14
Smitten

In a letter dated April 13, 1948, Gus tells his parents about an event that he doesn't realize will change his life forever.

> I was at a cocktail party a while ago where I had with me a very cute girl (Claire Thompson), really cute, she is not unlike Ingrid Bergman, and is a very good swimmer. She is involved in swimming. We got along really well and we are going to a big black tie party Saturday, and next Friday after that I am taking her to a big dance in Tacoma.

Gus proceeded to invite Claire to a Sigma Nu function called a House Party. The whole fraternity, including a married couple who are chaperones, were going to travel to a place that had cabins, tennis courts, riding trails and horses, soccer fields, and a swimming pool. (Gus had also promised to take Claire skiing.) After telling his parents about Claire, he wrote to his mother, in his usual teasing way said, "Now Mamma, my oh my, take it easy, it is only a little fluff in the wind." He continued, "I am going to travel to Alaska pretty soon, and will be gone 3½ months, so I can't be more than ½ engaged before I leave…enough about girls."

But it would not be enough about this *particular* girl. A month later, things had moved along.

> The girl I am together with now, her name is Claire (pronounced Kler) Thompson. She has English blood. I went down to watch her swimming exhibition. She hit her head in the bottom after diving in., bled a little and she was not feeling too well the whole evening at the black tie party, [was] tired after the swimming.

Gus goes on to tell his parents he and Claire are going to movies, playing tennis, and bike riding. He also wants to teach her how to ski properly. On a sweet note, he says, "She is knitting a bright red scarf for me, which I am going to use in the jumping hill next winter." It sounds like Gus was already making future plans with Claire!

What Gus didn't know was when he picked up Claire for dates at her sorority house; her house mates would constantly tease her. They would yell, "Claire, Guuuuustav is here." He also didn't know that Claire was dating other college boys in addition to Gus. In fact, sometimes she'd have more than one date in an evening. (The university had three men to every woman.) Over time, though, Gus became aware that he had competition, and wasn't happy about it. The story goes that he would sometimes hide in the bushes outside the sorority house to see who brought Claire home that night. (Of course, she was on curfew.) For a young man used to being the center of attention, that was quite understandable.

Around this time, Gus was gearing up to head up to Alaska again. He is flat broke, and hopes to make enough to carry him through the next year. Money and a scholarship were crucial for this hardworking college student. But there was no shortage of women. He tells his parents about many, many women he has met---Ruth, Carolyn, Betty to name a few---but Claire has grabbed his heart. Before he's leaving for Alaska, he describes a weekend he's about to embark on:

> We take off for Lake Crescent to be there for 2 days at our house party (50 boys with girls and chaperones) We are going to party, dance, play tennis, ping pong, baseball, horseback riding, and take a deep breath before the final exams. I am, of course, taking Claire.

Gus would have to leave his beloved Claire for another stint in Alaska. He had tremendous stamina and determination throughout this time. Fishing in Alaska, as it was before, was not easy. But Gus was willing to do whatever was required to get an education and become a successful citizen. Now, he would see if absence makes the heart grow fonder.

A young Claire Thompson.

Chapter 15
The Land Of The Midnight Sun

Gus arrived in Alaska this time on June 5th 1948, with $2.48 in his pocket. He left behind good final exam grades, and qualified for a much needed scholarship. There was a farewell party for him and his friend Kjell who was returning to Norway to work in the family business. Like many immigrants, there was an internal struggle to stay in a country they'd grown to love or return to the homeland. Kjell had a serious girlfriend and loved the University, nonetheless, he returned to Norway, while Gus headed north. Before Gus left, he confided to his parents that he and Claire would split the expense of dates. He said, "We are more like brother and sister, really good friends, nothing serious yet."

Gus was glad to leave the confines of his school and test himself again in the last great wilderness. He boarded the Phoenix X in Seattle, and after stocking supplies (including lumber) they set sail for Alaska. The ship was 80 feet long and 76 tons gross and the next fastest boat in a fleet of 14. He described it as a "Large barge full of logs in tow." The trip went well and took about three days. "From Seattle to Ketchikan [we] had beautiful weather, we hardly saw a wave on the whole trip, and brilliant sun." Gus got a good tan as his job was standing at the wheel to keep the boat on course according to the compass. The ship traveled through a vast array of wildlife. Gus wrote,

"We saw some big sharks (uhu)! I shook with the thought of falling overboard!! They swam right up to the boat." The engineer, not being a nature lover, fired two shots at one of them and got a hit. There were seals and porpoises that played around the boat. Gus described, "…some kind of whale they call black fish which has a fin 6 feet high, which sticks above the water." Of course, today we know the black fish as the killer whale.

They arrived in Ketchikan in the wee hours of the morning and managed to get a few hours of sleep. Soon after, there were orders to go to Bell Island Hot Springs, 40 miles north of Ketchikan and on Behm Canal. The springs were discovered centuries before by the native tribes and used for medicinal purposes. By the 1900's the people of Ketchikan started to venture in because it was reputed to have healing powers. Gus recalled that they needed to go because a captain and bookkeeper with the company were sick. Gus remembered it this way:

> It was an idyllic little place completely isolated deep into one of the fjords. These hot springs were supposed to provide some miracles against arthritis. I took a bath there, but what a horrible smell, worse than rotten eggs. Well, folks even sat and drank some of that water.

The goal for Gus was to make as many overtime hours that he could. His work ethic was contagious; he had hooked four of his fraternity brothers into to coming up to work with him. In the evenings, they would while away the hours playing bridge or deep in conversation…young men with youthful dreams. As was the case the previous year, Gus raved about the food: steak, crab, chicken, pork chops, all kinds of fruit, banana cream pies and a variety of cakes. These men were doing tough work that required thousands of calories.

In one of Gus's letters to home he wrote from a sunny deck while listening to music from California. Sometimes night would melt into day with their uneven work schedule. "One thing I have learned is that there is nothing like regular hours any time of day or night. Sometimes we have to stay up all night long, and they wake us up any time when we arrive at a harbor." Being outside, though, meant catching sight of some rare occurrences in nature, "A few days ago there was a big whale which was completely white, a really beautiful sight, too bad I did not have my camera handy."

On land, there were other kinds of adventure, especially when you mix boys away from home and the 4th of July:

> We had a big party in Ketchikan. Of course, everybody was in town, and lot of folks were drunk, and there were many fights. The 5th we had a towing competition between "Jack B" and our boat "Phoenix X". The "Jack B" is almost twice as heavy and has two propellers (we have one) and they have 230 HP, we have 220. There

was a bet that they could pull us backwards while we were going full speed forward. The whole thing took place in front of the city dock which was crowded full of people. To many's surprise we won, we pulled "Jack B" backwards instead. We have now proven that we have the strongest and fastest boat in the whole fleet up here.

Alaska was also the land of Gold Fever. For a poor, struggling student like Gus, hitting the jackpot was not far from his mind.

Today I took a trip to an old gold mine which has been shut down. We picked up several rocks which contain a little gold in them, but mostly copper. I found a very special big rock which shines from gold and copper. If it does not get too heavy I'll send you a tiny rock home with one of the letters, so you can see what they look like.

After a long period of no mail, Gus hit gold when a letter from a special someone arrived. "Claire tells me that she is coming with her family up here to Ketchikan on a trip at the end of August. They are going to be here in Ketchikan only 6 hours, so it is almost 90 % sure that I will be out on a trip at that time, but time will show."

As much as Gus was excited by the prospect of seeing Claire, there's another letter, too. This one was from Carolyn Teren. Gus had met her in Sun Valley. Carolyn came from a highly successful and wealthy Portland family. In fact, her grandfather, Henry Pittock, was a pioneer publisher and editor of the *Oregonian.* The Pittock Mansion still stands today in Portland, Oregon and is a historical landmark. In his letter, Gus writes:

> Carolyn tells me that she is surely coming to Salt Lake City next winter to watch the American ski jumping championships and specially to meet me. She says she is coming to watch me win! So there! She is really a funny girl, she sends me all kinds of funny things in the letters. If I have mentioned that I had cut my hand, she promptly sends me band aids etc. so I mostly get funny things.

At this point, we don't find out yet if Gus sees Claire in Alaska, but he does share more about her with his parents in a later letter. There's a real sense of ambivalence, maybe because he doesn't want to get his hopes up.

> I can tell you a little bit about Claire, if you are interested. She, together with 4 other girls (ladies) are responsible for a large camp for young children (250!!), something like camping and scout camp, where she also is instructor in swimming. She is studying Norwegian every day (poor girl!), why, I do not know. She is knitting a scarf for me which is supposed to "help" me to win the championships title next year.

Fortunately, there is nothing serious between us, we are more or less playmates.

During this time in Alaska, Gus came across an amazing piece of German history, the *Haida*. "One day I saw the famous American yacht *Haida* which was named Yacht of the year. Gus was clearly impressed. "It is 165 feet long and cost $ 3 million!! It really was a sight!" The yacht was originally built in a German shipyard in the Keil harbor. In 1946, it was actually renamed "Sarina" even though Gus still referred to it as *Haida*. It changed wealthy hands several time, but was refurbished and renamed *Haida B* and restored to her original condition. Remarkably, the old girl is still in service today.

As the days grew longer, the sun would shine brighter for Gus that summer. Many opportunities were just beyond the horizon.

Gus in Alaska.

Chapter 16
A Job Well Done

August in Alaska was beautiful that summer, and Gus couldn't be happier. "They say it hasn't been such nice weather in Ketchikan for 40 years." His financial future was also full of sunshine. His knowledge of accounting and initiative paid off. The excitement in this letter is palpable.

> I have been promoted to assistant bookkeeper at Sunny Point Cannery, and I'm very happy about that!!!! We came in to the dock late last evening, and I went up early this morning to wash clothes and take a shower, and met Mr. Fritz Frolich, Superintendent, on the way up, and he said quite calmly (in English). "Have you been up to the head bookkeeper and talked to him about the new job you have gotten" I almost fell on my ... and rushed up to the office, and that was the truth!! I think the salary now is $ 330 per month, and that is damn fantastic (to say it straight out!!), in addition, the job is along my field of study. I will now sit behind a desk with a chair, which I can tilt. On the desk are two telephones, 3 - 4 ink pots, pens, pencils, several machines which can add, subtract and divide, and at the side there is a small table with a typewriter.

Gus went from a deck hand to a lovely office with "…rugs on the floor here in my room, one large and three small, yes I even have a telephone!" The job had great possibilities; they were so impressed with him that they wanted him back every summer, and to work even in Seattle. Whatever the future would hold, Gus was clearly over the moon. "This whole thing hit me like a bomb, and you can't believe how happy I am!!"

Gus (at left) working at Sunny Pt. Cannery, 1948.

Throughout his time in Alaska, Gus was still hearing from is friend Carolyn Teren. In the following letter, he reassured his mother he was not about to tie the knot with Carolyn or anybody.

> You don't have to worry that I am going to get married soon, Mamma. My plans are not to get married before I have my completed degree in my pocket. I am not

going to do anything in a hurry. So far I have met so many girls of every kind, so it is easier to see which ones are of value and which are not. I am very guarded with regards to girls, because over here you don't know what kind of people one can run into, but they don't fool me (I think, anyway). Many girls have told me that they don't understand why a famous man like me is not married or engaged. I thank them for the compliment.

Throughout the summer, things were not always easy in Alaska. "Up here lately it has been such terrible storms that people can't remember that it has ever been so bad. We had a lot of damage since 16 of the 22 traps were damaged, we got some of them repaired, but we had a big setback, several boats capsized and several people drowned."

Gus ended his time in Alaska on a high note. Weathering all kinds of challenges, he had proved himself to be adaptable and capable; he had managed to make it through two summers, and even ended up with a big promotion. This was a can-do-attitude that would serve him well. Ready for the next chapter at the University of Washington, Gus wrote the following letter on the plane on route to Seattle.

Now I am up in the air again on my way to Seattle. I was boss for one day at the plant, and had the feeling that everything depended on me. It was a really great

Summer I had this year with regards to work, girls, wine and song. Not a drink since July 5th. But if I get the job again next summer depends on the auditors i.e. if they find too many errors in the payroll, not everybody are without mistakes, but if I have over paid anybody I have to go around and collect. Time will show. I met a very nice girl there, and we had a lot of fun together at the movies, dancing, and mostly in her home. I figure to have $1,050 in my pocket when I arrive in Seattle. I will now have 2 days' vacation i.e. parties and fun and reunion joy.

Chapter 17
My Girl

After the second great Alaskan adventure, Gus arrived back in Seattle and hit the ground running. In October, he wrote to his parents about a long weekend with his "other" girlfriend, Carolyn Teren from Portland. Gus had an on and off romance with her. Carolyn has fond memories of Gus and Sun Valley. She said, "I remember dancing with Gus at the Duchin Room." The Duchin Room was reportedly named after Marjorie Duchin, wife of Eddy Duchin who was a famous pianist and bandleader from the 1930's and 40's. Carolyn added, "Gus was always so nice."

Carolyn came from a fabulously rich family; for Gus it was a whole different world. The Teren family was quite well-known in the Portland area. Nils Teren, Carolyn's father, owned paper mills in Oregon. Here was a young man who was as poor as a church mouse meeting one of the wealthiest families in the northwest. When Carolyn invited Gus to her family home in Oregon, he wrote to his parents with great enthusiasm.

> I was graciously received by the family, who lived in a giant house (huge, with lots of trees and lawn etc.) We dressed for dinner, which was delicious. Then Carolyn and I went to the theater and saw a beautiful operetta

(tickets were paid in advance) The Desert Song. Her daddy gave me his keys to his Chrysler!

She also took Gus to their summer home. "That is one of the most fantastic places I have seen. It has 4-5 different buildings, which all are made of logs which were cut when the place was cleared. The main building was huge and built with lots of character, really beautiful." After they went to the summer place, Carolyn and Gus met with Hjalmar Hvam and his wife, Vera. Hvam was originally from Kongsberg, but made quite a name for himself in America. During the 1930's, he was the most dominant downhill and cross country ski racer in the Pacific Northwest. He would also become famous for inventing the world's first workable safety ski binding. During this trip, Gus was able to visit Timberline Lodge, a jewel of a resort that still stands today.

But throughout this time, Claire was a constant in Gus's life. It was another era back when romance was in the air, and relationships remained for the most part wholesome. When he wrote to his parents not long after, he wrote about of a special picture he'd sent them. It turned out Claire did visit him while he was in Alaska. "The other is of Claire and me taken by Claire's mother near Sunny Point Cannery, when she was up here this summer." It took a lot for Claire to travel thousands of miles, just for a short visit.

By December of 1948, Claire was mentioned in most of Gus's letters home. He also wrote about his demanding schedule:

> So far I have already had 160 jumps. I can get a chance to represent Norway in the World Championships in 1950 in Lake Placid, USA. The first competition I will take part in is in Lake Placid, then in Rossland, Canada Jan. 8, then Mt. Baker, Washington, then 2 competitions in Seattle, then Leavenworth, then Spokane, then McCall (Pacific Northwest Championships), then Salt Lake City (American Championships, the big one), then Portland, Seattle, Walla Walla, Seattle, Pullman, Anthony Lakes, perhaps a trip to Reno again this year. As you can see it is a pretty big program. I am going to represent only the University this year (new rules).

That Christmas, Gus was invited to an all-expense paid trip to Sun Valley. Gus described his time there as being treated like royalty. Carolyn and Claire were both there too. Even though Gus danced and dined with Carolyn, he eagerly awaited Claire's arrival. He wrote:

> Claire and I are more or less in love. I have bought a Christmas present for Claire, it is a pair of ski mittens, because she lost hers skiing when we were up in the mountain. In addition, I promised her one of my scarves. She knitted a very nice bright red scarf for me, which I use when jumping, and now she is starting on a pair of socks for me. She is very domestic and clever.

The only disappointment of the trip was he finally saw the movie, "That Wonderful Urge." (The film that he'd hoped to be in.) He wrote his parents, "The movie was a great disappointment! Almost all the scenes from Sun Valley were cut. All the others who had also been in the movie were also disappointed that they did not see themselves in the film." But the good news, by New Year's, Gus declared Claire as "My girl" to his parents.

Chapter 18
Love Is In The Air

By the beginning of the New Year, Claire was not only Gus's girl, she was his one and only. It's best to read what he told his mother in his own words in a letter dated January 26th:

I am very much in love at the moment. Claire and I are swooning and swooning. We have been together almost one year now, and it has developed from friendship to more or less being in love. Honestly, if I did not have any studies left, I could easily get married tomorrow. Don't have a stroke, Mamma, I am not married yet, and do not plan to before I have finished my studies. I just want to tell you how things are going, so you can be part of it and follow along. Times can change, but the way the case is now, I am very much in love. I feel so happy, so when I am jumping I feel that I have something extra to jump for, and when I get back home from the ski trips I am looking forward to seeing her again. She is very domestic, loves to cook, and loves children. She is studying children's thinking etc. at the university, and during the summer she is in charge of a large children's camp outside Seattle. She has recently started with the ski sport, which I try to teach her a little about, she plays tennis with me, she is good at horseback riding, and loves the outdoors, does not smoke and only drinks socially.

Gus & Claire, 1949.

The following months were a whirlwind of ski competitions and college classes. Gus was holding his own in both. "The official who stood at the take-off said that he did not think I would go over 60 meter in my second jump based on the speed I had on the take-off, but I really hit it with all I had. I got a trophy about 40 cm tall. Claire called me long distance the evening before to wish me good luck!!"

And in romance Gus was getting an A+. In this letter to his parents, dated March 3, 1949, Gus confided that he's taken a big step with Claire. "Claire and I are half engaged now, I am going to give her my fraternity pin, and when she wears that it means that she is pinned, something they consider half engaged. We are as happy as we can be."

By March 18th the ski season was winding down. Gus felt good about where he was by then. "It will be the end of the jumping competitions when I now get back to the university. It has been a wonderful as well as educational jumping season. It has brought me to the thought that I have to train like mad to keep up with the boys back home." But before it ended, he was able to go to fabulous Banff in British Columbia.

> Banff was a beautiful, small place, lots of modern hotels, and many possibilities as a winter sports resort, with a big ski lift etc. All the people were extra friendly, they took endless pictures of us, and we signed numerous autographs. We were invited to use the famous Banff Hot Springs free of charge. In the evening we were invited to a big party at a well-known scientist from Los Angeles.

The minute Gus got home from the trip, he was on his way to Tacoma to see his beloved Claire. "I learned to know her parents better, and they are really sweet. I lived there 2 days. The last day I was there Thompson drove us out to their summer place, where he cooked a good steak dinner. Claire and I did sun tanning down on the beach, played ping- pong, and played cards."

Throughout this time, Gus was anxious to get his parent's blessing regarding Claire. "I am happy to hear that you are pleased with Claire's appearance. I am sure you will like her so much better when you meet her." It's understandable that they're cautious about their son proposing to an American woman. They only expected their son to go to America for a short time, now he's enrolled full-time in a university and talking marriage to a foreigner. His correspondence is filled with his new life with Claire's and the Thompson family:

> I had a very nice Easter with the Thompsons in Tacoma. The Friday before Easter Sigma Nu had a barn dance, where we had fun with beer and dancing. We traveled out to Thompson's summer place, where Claire, her mother and I went golfing, something I have never done before, but I did not do too badly, because I beat her mother one time and Claire both times. They have played quite a bit of golf before. After golf we went back to the summer place, where Thompson had cooked great lamb chops, for dessert we had strawberries with cream. Claire and I washed dishes, and we studied a little. About 10 PM we drove back to Tacoma. The next morning was Easter Sunday. We had a delicious breakfast, and then the whole family went to church, think I was in church for the first time since I came here. That did not hurt, and the minister had a short sermon. In the afternoon Claire and I drove around the outskirts of Tacoma and out in the country and looked at the country side and the new houses there. Later we visited some friends, and before we knew it we had to return to Seattle. For Easter Claire and I gave Mrs. Thompson a nice potted plant, and she gave me a fountain pen which can write in three different colors.

Claire's family lived a comfortable life. Her father, Lindsay (L.L.) Thompson was a former Washington State Attorney General, and at this time had a successful law firm. The Thompson family owned a summer home on Vashon Island, a northwest jewel. The mountain views and clear, cold water delighted Gus and probably reminded him of his homeland.

On April 13th Gus's world was rocked in a whole different way; a 7.1 magnitude earthquake shook Washington State; eight people were killed and dozens were injured. Fortunately, Gus was safe, but a bit perplexed by all the fuss. Perhaps after surviving a war in his homeland, this seemed more like an inconvenience.

> It lasted about 2 minutes, and shook the buildings a little bit. I sat and studied in the big university library, suddenly the whole large building started to dance around. Small pieces of white plaster fell from the ceiling, it squeaked in the timbers, and the light fixtures were swaying back and forth. All the students rushed outside, and then it was all over. It wasn't much to talk about at all, aside from some older buildings down town failed, and some tall chimneys fell down and hit a few people in the head. It had a much worse effect on Olympia (a neighbor town).

Gus had hoped to make a trip home, but he quickly realized it might take him several years to leave Norway. There was no way he would leave Claire behind for that long. Besides, his job prospects were far better in the U.S., in fact he was due to leave for Alaska a third time. School continued to be a tremendous challenge, but each time Gus would come out better than he thought. "Right now I am taking the most difficult course in Accounting which consists of problems when a firm owns another firm which again owns a third firm, which again owns a small portion of the first firm, and how to keep the books. We had interim exam the other day and I had the third highest grade in the class."

Gus was not the only athlete in the relationship. Claire was quite accomplished in sports, especially swimming. Throughout her entire life Claire enjoyed the water. (Years later, well into her 70's, she would swim and fish at the Raaum summer cabin in Allyn, WA.) But in those younger times, Gus was clearly impressed with her youthful exuberance in the "Silver Fishes" synchronized swim team.

> This evening Claire is in a big swimming exhibition. You know such show where they make formation in unison in the water, and make out different figurations, and almost dance to the music, there are about 20 girls involved, and it is sold out all 4 evening shows. Claire is president of this group.

Throughout this time, Gus is writing diligently to his parents. You can hear in his words the need for them to love and accept his choice for a wife. Time and distance were great barriers for the young couple.

> Claire was really extra excited about your letter, Mamma. She has read it at least 20 times, and she has shown the pictures to all possible people she knows, she has them with her all the time. She really liked the letter very much, and only hopes to get a chance to meet you soon, something I also am looking forward to very much.

Gus continued to excel in school and beyond. He was initiated into an exclusive group called the Oval Club. They picked only 46 men out of 7,000 who were outstanding in sports and grades. Gus also received a much needed scholarship for the whole next year, which saved him $300…a lot of money then. Gus was also saving money to buy his girl an engagement ring. It was a bit disconcerting for him that unlike Norway where a gold ring sufficed, in America, women expected a diamond. "I will work most of the time so I can save some. Now I have a chance to buy a gorgeous diamond ring." With his expenses, studies, work and activities, Gus really couldn't do much for his parents, but in his letters home…his heart was always in the right place.

> Remember, if it is anything Pappa needs to eat or something you cannot get in Norway, write to me immediately! Then I'll see if I can take care of it, there

is always a way out. We got back our accounting midterm today which covered the most difficult material within this field, and I had the highest grade (A) in the whole class of over 80 students!! I was proud, and the professor pointed towards me, and told everybody that I was the best man. In English I got back the long report and got a B and that was fine. In track I was on the winning relay team (800 m), and we were photographed etc.

The new couple was always on the go. That year they went with Gus's fraternity house on an annual weekend trip to a big resort. They played tennis, went out in a motor boat, played baseball, and billiards all in one afternoon. Sixty couples attended. It seems it was a simpler, more romantic time in those days. America was at peace, and so was life for Gus and Claire. The world was their oyster during that magic weekend:

> In the evening we went up to the hot springs where we swam, then we danced a little, and loved in the moonlight. Next morning Claire and I went out rowing, played a little tennis and had a great horseback ride up along a trail far up in the hills. I am getting pretty good at riding now. We galloped full speed along open stretches, and it was indescribable fun, just like cowboys.

With the Thompsons', Gus found a new family and acceptance---even with his thick Norwegian accent. Lindsay Thompson was hesitant at first about his daughter's choice, but it's clear from Gus's letters, the family embraced him: "We just had 3 days' vacation, and I was down to Claire's summer place again with her family, and had a wonderful combination of exercise (wood chopping), studying, and rest. One dinner we had fried chicken and fresh strawberries!"

During this time of correspondence, Gus pays his greatest tribute to his parents. Not only had they reared a star athlete and fine student, but a son who viewed them as the model when it came to the biggest decision of his life. "If I get a wife like you have been to Papa, I shall cry from happiness!! I have you two as the most shining example for the ideal couple. I hope to God that Claire and I will be as happy."

Chapter 19
Alaska By Sea

In the summer of 1949, Gus embarked on his third trek to the last frontier. That year, however, he didn't fly but traveled on a yacht. This was the beginning of another big adventure. The yacht had 430 horsepower, two propellers, and nice cabin with a birds eye view. Down below were beds, a dining/bridge table with deep chairs, a small kitchen with refrigerator, and bathroom. They also had a radio and telephone to stay in touch with other boats and with the cannery at Sunny Point. At first it was smooth sailing, but the trip definitely had some challenges. In reading Gus's account of the trek, I'm sure his parents were relieved to read about it *after* the fact:

> We had beautiful weather the first day and traveled at about 15 knots. In the evening we filled gasoline from one of the cannery tenders, and then went to bed. You see we cannot travel at night, since there is so much stuff drifting on the ocean (logs etc.), and if we would hit one of those while we are traveling at full speed, it would knock a hole in the hull, and we would sink right away, or at least bend the propellers. Usually we start at 4 AM to catch up with the cannery tender, which was supposed to look after us to make sure we would make it OK to Alaska in good shape, besides they had our gasoline supply on board. When we were half ways, however, we had used up all the gasoline which some idiot had calculated would last us the whole trip. We

therefore had to borrow money from the crew on the cannery tender so we could buy gasoline in Canada. We use 26 liters gas per Norwegian mile, so you understand these two engines use gasoline, and the distance from Seattle to Ketchikan is 100 Norwegian miles. In addition we used 8 liter of oil per day and lots of water. Our fog horn malfunctioned, likewise our electric pump and fan, and lastly our fresh water system plugged up. All in all we had a fine, very exciting trip, once in a while we ran into bad weather with very bad rip tide. The waves rushed completely over the boat, and we had leaks several places. You see the yacht has been built too light, and can't stand so much shaking. We broke some dishes, but not too badly. Jack and I traded off steering, and I for the most part was responsible for the food preparation. To get away from the rip tides we went closer to shore, but we suddenly started to hit bottom because it was very shallow, so we were afraid of damaging the props. Since the fresh water system was not working and we had a leak in our freshwater tank for one engine, we could only run one engine until we came into Canadian port for gas and repairs. Since the wind and the waves were so strong, we could not make any progress, so we had to fill the tank with salt water, and raced to the next Canadian port, to make some repairs and to flush out the tank. Since I had not planned to be in Canada when we left, I did not have with me my passport, but fortunately the Canadian authorities did not ask to see my passport, so we lucked out. We ran into terrible fog where you could not see 50 feet, but Jack was an excellent navigator.

Once the two men arrived in Ketchikan, they were greeted by a happy anxious crowd from their job. Of course, the first thing Gus did was check his mail, and there was a letter from his beloved Claire. Another bit of good news was he landed a new job until fishing started. The sea had always called to Gus, and for a while he could be captain of a snazzy ship, called the *Fritzie*:

> I am the captain of the yacht, i.e. all the papers will state that I am the "driver" of the yacht, but I think I have to be an American citizen to get these papers and to make sure the insurance coverage is OK, but I don't know anything about that yet. My job is to maintain the yacht, so everything shines on board, fill oil and gasoline, change oil, fill water tanks, and keep the engines in top shape, so it is ready to go at any time. Today I have washed the whole cabin with kitchen, WC, and polished the furniture, so it is shining like the sun. In addition I greased the engines and changed oil, and had a machinist to handle some more technical repairs. When I am finished with the boat, then it will shine like newly polished silver. I don't know what my wages are yet, but I am hoping for the best. When we are going out, it will be me at the wheel, and controls and at the compass. I hope everything will go OK, because the boat costs something like $ 60,000 (NK 300,000!) so I don't want to damage it. When the cannery starts then I will have the same job I had last year. Now I have a small, nice room with bed (sofa

pull-out), table, chair, lamp, a small closet and a sink, and I am satisfied with that.

Gus also received a nice letter from Claire's father. (He had definitely won his future father-in-law over.) In the letter, Mr. Thompson told Gus he missed his help chopping wood at the summer place. He also encouraged Gus to fly down on a weekend and fill up the woodshed. Gus shared with his parents that Claire's father "… earns about $ 10,000 per year, and that is fairly normal here, when you have 4 in a family, of which two girls attend the university, and have to be dressed in modern clothes as the fashion changes." Gus went on to speculate good-naturedly, "He is probably looking forward to the day when I can lift these expenses off his shoulders by marrying Claire."

That year, fishing was delayed until August. Gus was concerned that he would not earn more than $1,000 that summer unless his boss changed his wages. He vowed that if he were to return, he'd rather take a job as a mate on one of the boats, "Because I can earn a lot more than I do in the office, and the money means a lot more for me." With his plans to marry Claire, money was definitely a priority. And besides, the job he has was, in his words, "boring."

The brightest spots in that summer were hearing from Claire. Her care packages were particularly welcomed. "Yesterday I received a nice package from Claire. She had baked a good portion of delicious cookies, which I have here on my desk. They taste very good, so I think I will sign her up!!" As Gus describes in the rest of this letter, life on land and sea wasn't a piece of cake.

> Here in Alaska we have been working around the clock, practically speaking. We have gotten unusually large quantities of salmon this year. One day we had as many as 220,000 salmon at one time, which were made into 10,000 cases (at 24 Kg.) of canned salmon. We usually start at 6 AM and keep going until 12 - 1 - 2 in the morning, and since we only have one shift all workers get pretty well worn out. Some of them have only had 2 hours sleep each night during the whole week.

The separation from Claire could be challenging, too, in that she was pretty independent herself. Not only was it uncommon for women to be at universities, but Claire also liked to travel. In one of his letters, Gus shared his reservations: "Claire has plans for a bicycle trip in Europe next summer. Several of her friends are presently on such a trip this summer, so they can give her good advice. However, the plans are very new, and I do not like that she would travel without my masculine protection."

Thankfully by September 22nd, Gus was free to leave Alaska. The season was over, and none too soon. The weather was so bad; no planes were able to land. Instead, Gus traveled on the Prince George, a Canadian ship. He described it as a new hyper modern passenger boat. After a rough passage over windy seas, he landed in Vancouver BC and took the train to Seattle. In his own words, "It is going to be nice to get back to Claire and the University."

On board the Fritzie.

Chapter 20
Torn Between Two Countries

With being so far from home, one of the most difficult times for Gus was when his father took a terrible fall. Even after five months, his father was still in bad shape. He ended up being hospitalized, and had a long and painful recovery. Decades later, Dick Raaum recalled that their father never *really* fully recovered; it was an enormous setback. The accident brought on a depression that would haunt their father for the rest of his life. In a letter (10/8/1949) to his father, you can hear Gus's concern:

> It was so sad to hear that you had to take another month off due to your health, but you expect too much from yourself. Pappa, Rome cannot be built in one day. It is much better to wait one month now, and live in peace and quiet, in good health the rest of your life, instead of overdoing it now.

Gus's life was moving along in both positive and negative terms. The good news was he was doing well in school, had quit his restaurant job and secured a new job correcting tests for an accounting professor at the University. Gus noted, "He was new here, so he did not know anybody, therefore I went after him like an arrow. We got along fine, and he gave me the position." This opportunity was much more in line with what Gus hoped to do after school. As would be his way, he was also working at The Seattle Times correcting guessing games at $1 an hour, earning about $5 a week.

In school, Gus continued to show the same work ethic he had with jobs. He poured himself into mastering the English language and it continued to pay off. "In English composition writing I surprised myself greatly by the fact that one composition was read out loud in class as a good example, and hang on, it was my work! That is fun particularly in a class with 30 American students." It seemed that there wasn't an opportunity too great or too small that Gus didn't go for. "I took an admissions test for Beta Alpha Psi, which is a division of a National Accounting Fraternity. You remember that I tried this last spring and did not make it, and I don't know if I made it today either. This has nothing to do with the University, but it gives a certain amount of prestige."

Although Gus was back in the swing of things after coming home from Alaska, he and Claire were going through a period of uncertainty. It's easy to see how torn Gus is between his homeland and the love of his life.

> Claire and I are no longer pinned, even though we are still very good buddies as before. We talked about how everything was so uncertain with me with regards to me staying here in USA, with military service etc., so we realized that it was better that we were not dependent

> upon another. If anything comes in the way, it is more than enough to take care of one's self. There is no question in my mind that it is her that I want, but we thought this was the best move for both of us. I am still with her at every opportunity and am teaching her Norwegian which she is very interested in. Time will show the relationship between us. It is very possible I will be coming home on a trip next fall.

Going home was a recurring theme in much of Gus's correspondence. On one hand, he was meeting with a lot of success in America, but he probably had some level of guilt that his parents might need his help. Not only did he miss them, he missed his homeland. Then, the possibility of going to Norway came up with one of his professors.

> My wonderful professor Cannon, who I have in auditing, gave me a lot of courage a while ago when I went to his office to ask him some questions. He asked me if I would like to get a stipend which consisted of free travel, stay and expenses for one year in any country I wanted to study and to take part in the social life as a representative from USA to develop friendships with other countries. I can't believe that they would send a Norwegian citizen as a representative of the USA.

The professor had even nominated Gus for this post, but it was not to be. It turned out, the position required US citizenship. Once again, Gus was advised not to leave this country. There was a strong chance, once he got there, he would not be able to leave Norway. On top of this, he struggled with losing the person he loved more than anything else.

> Claire is pessimistic because she is afraid that she is admiring me, and is looking up to me due to my sports results, my good grades, and because (as they say) I am popular, she is afraid that it is not love to the bottom of her heart. There is no doubt in my soul, so I am not going to see her or phone her for quite a while now, and will go out with other girls, to try to open her eyes. It is time to find out one way or another.

Chapter 21
A Season Of Joy

Football season, the holidays and young love were in full swing in November of 1949. Gus was getting an education in football rivalry when he and his pals drove down to Portland to watch a football game between University of Washington and University of Oregon. There were at least 1,500 students from UW who watched this rivalry. It was a great game, people went wild and when their team left the field with a victory, they almost tore down the stands. They ran on the field to tear down one of the goal posts to cut up and take a piece home as a souvenir. But the posts were made of steel and sat in concrete, so they were unsuccessful. Afterwards there were plenty of drunken brawls. Three guys were about to take Gus on, but he was standing with Claire, so they didn't touch him. Gus left Claire with her parents, and went back to the car where his friends Gunnar, Jan and Ben waited. On the way there, Gus was attacked by three guys from Univ. of Oregon. They snatched his Husky cap, and tried to run away. Because Gus was in excellent shape, he ran after him, but things got a bit dicey after that.

> I caught the guy who had my cap, and at the same time accidentally tore his beautiful sweater in two, he then threw my cap over my head to one of the other two guys, after which I hit him, so he lost my cap, so I

snapped it up from the street, and ran like h... back to the car to get some help from Gunnar, Jan and Ben, because in the meantime another 8-10 guys had come to help the three guys who were after me. When they arrived, they saw us four broad shouldered guys standing there, they cooled off, and one of the guys came over to me with the tail between his legs to apologize, but I did not shake his hand, and told him to go to hell, and beat it, before I beat you up. They left in a hurry. It was a fun experience.

Gus and Claire were back to seeing each other again. That evening, after the game they went out to a big nightclub where Sigma Nu had made reservations for 30 couples. They had a great orchestra, drinks, and a very lively evening. "The whole gang sang familiar songs the whole evening, and the mood was on top." After staying out until the wee hours of the morning, Gus and Claire headed back to Seattle. There's no doubt from what he writes to his parents, that they are once again a couple.

It was a marvelous weekend all the way through. That was probably the last chance to have such a big evening. We have three days off from the University due to Holidays. This evening Claire has invited me to the Pledge dance they are having at the sorority where she lives. Tomorrow Claire and I are going on the drive to Canada. You see, she has her mother's car for 14 days, because her mother is in Chicago for a Girl Scout national meeting.

Gus and his friend, Gunnar, spent Thanksgiving with the Thompson family in Tacoma. Gus was thrilled to eat a marvelous home-cooked meal. "The dinner, which always consists of turkey with all the trimmings, soup, vegetables, wine, beer, desert, whiskey, and coffee, was very delicious and also formal. We three lived at Claire's 2 days."

Whatever doubts Claire and Gus might have had, they dissipated that November. In the crisp fall air, and with Christmas around the corner, their love blossomed. Gus made their plans known to his parents in one of his letters. There's a sense of closure as he lets his mother know there's no turning back.

> I regret, Mamma, but I have to put the small stone back on your heart, because the relationship between Claire and me at the moment is wonderful. Everything is all clear in all directions, so it is very possible that we will be engaged before too long (get a hold of yourself, Mamma!) She is the most wonderful wife I could get, Mamma, even though she speaks English! I have not planned on settling in Norway anyway, so that problem will not be there. I hope to earn so much money that I can take a trip to Norway often! It is so terribly long since I have seen you last!!!!! My future is without doubt in America, I only wish you could meet Claire! Everybody is really jealous, and say that I have the most wonderful girl I could find (I know that). I may

also be able to afford to bring you both over here on a trip, even though that will take a little time.

By December, Gus had his passport and visa extended until January, 1951. He was also applying for jobs to get ready for a very big event:

> I am going to start applying for a good position now, so everything is ready by this fall. I also have small plans to get married next fall, dear parents; you have to try to take it in good spirits. I have worked on the side and have saved money for an engagement ring, so the bomb could go off at any time. I only regret that you have never seen Claire, but this can be corrected in the near future.

Before they would marry, Gus was hoping to go up to Alaska one more time, and save up at least $1200. He and Claire had started to shop for engagement rings. They were considering an antique gold ring with a diamond. "It is a giant step and a huge expense ($ 300), so we'll see what we decide. We also looked at silver and ceramics, many beautiful things, especially the prices!"

Christmas time brought joy and a bit of nostalgia, "I really hope you had a wonderful Christmas Eve at home and Dick in Sweden." It had been a long time since Gus had seen his parents, but even longer when it came to his beloved brother. They would not meet again for quite a while. Fortunately, Gus had skiing and the Thompson family to distract him. "We stayed at the cabin for 5 days and trained hard in jumping and cross-country, and went to Seattle, then on to Tacoma." Gus jumped right into all the American holiday traditions with his future in-laws.

> We helped Thompson set up and decorate the Christmas tree on the 23rd, and we then went to town to buy Christmas presents. Gunnar, Jan and I went in the toy department, and looked at electric trains and Christmas dwarfs and enjoyed ourselves. I bought Claire a blouse and 2 scarves, and gave her a picture of me (which was not very good) To Mrs. Thompson I brought 12 red carnations, which she was very happy about. Of course, on Christmas Eve it was a lot of activities with all kinds of preparation everywhere, and I helped as best I could. In most families over here, they do not open the Christmas presents until Christmas Day in the morning. However, Gunnar and I went to church Christmas Eve. Claire and her sister sang in the choir, it was very touching. I thought about us who always went to church together at home Christmas Eve. After church we drove back to Claire's house and had a nice time. Christmas Eve afternoon Gunnar, Jan and I went to a Scandinavian restaurant and ate rice pudding, julecake, flatbread with goat cheese, and had 2 beers, something we had not tasted for 3 years (except the beer) It really tasted very good, it was our little private

dinner. Claire tried to bake fattigmann, and did a nice job.

The Christmas of '49 was a delightful season for the soon-to-be engaged couple. That year, Claire incorporated some of the many Norwegian holiday traditions that would continue throughout their long marriage. Gus had clearly found the warm, family embrace he needed as he closed his Christmas letter. "At 5 PM we ate Christmas dinner at Thompson's, 12 at the table. Right afterwards we ski jumpers had to withdraw, to travel back to Seattle and up to the mountains after a very nice Christmas!!!"

Chapter 22
New Year, New Decade, New Life

Gus and Claire rang in the New Year with a big party of 60 people. Gus had a very important job, "I was in charge of the punch bowl and served drinks." At midnight, 1950 began in the U.S., but Gus didn't forget his country's celebration. "Gunnar and I celebrated also at 3 PM same afternoon New Year's Eve, because it was then New Year's Eve in Norway. It was a great party." However, the weather wasn't as great; icy roads kept Gus from getting to Seattle for ski-jumping try-outs. Fortunately, he got another chance and was in fine form.

The New Year sealed their love with an announcement, Gus wrote, "Here comes the bomb!! Claire and I are going to get engaged officially, Sunday January 15th!" Gus was thrilled to tell his parents how it all unfolded. "Claire and I went down to look at the ring, and the well-known jeweler (Gundersen) had made a special ring in antique gold with a diamond for Claire." The jeweler was a Thompson family friend so he made Gus a great deal and made Claire a happy bride-to-be. "She selected the special one which is an original, since it is the only one of its kind in the USA! I paid cash $ 252.76, and got the ring fitted exactly to Claire's finger."

While Claire planned a surprise party to celebrate with her friends, Gus handed out cigars at the Sigma Nu house to all the guys. The announcement appeared in the newspaper. (For a change, it wasn't about skiing awards.) At the time, Gus wrote, "We are planning to get married in October or there about. She possibly has a chance to come to Norway this summer on a bicycle trip if everything works out. Then you get to see her and get to know her." This turned out to be wishful thinking; Claire wasn't able to take the trip. But Gus is always optimistic, "There is no doubt in my mind that within a few years I will be able to save enough money to be able to come to Norway with Claire, and then it will be talking, hugging, and fun 24 hours per day!"

The ensuing months brought more excitement; wedding plans, academics and competition. In April of 1950, Gus traveled with his team to Denver in a DC-6 with 85 passengers. This was a pivotal time in the aeronautic industry. The DC-6 was intended as a military transport near the end of World War II but was eventually reworked for long-range commercial transport. For a young Norwegian like Gus, it was a heady time to be flying all over the country. The flight to Denver took five hours, and then the team drove into the mountains. Gus was living the *high* life, "Believe it or not, but we lived at 3,000 meters altitude---higher than Galhopiggen." This is the highest mountain in Norway, Sweden and Northern Europe. Gus describes the accommodations: "We lived in small cabins, two to every cabin. There was no heat or running water, so it wasn't exactly 1st class. The air was so thin up there that we could barely get any air in our lungs."

The next day the team drove to the downhill course at the Arapahoe Basin; an Alpine ski area in the Rocky Mountains in the White River National Forest. The run had a vertical drop of 1,000 meters. This is how it started for Gus:

A lift took us all the way to the top where we should start. The first few times down we took it easy to look over the course, later we took it non-stop down under control. The course was fairly easy, thank goodness. Then came Friday when the downhill race was held. I had [the] start number 6 out of 50 racers, which was the best start number for our team. The coach (Buster Campbell) thought I could go fast and do well, if I could stand up. I started, but went too fast in the upper and most difficult part of the course, with a sharp turn to the left, so I missed the turn, and flew through the air, up-side down, and landed on my head in the deep snow, off the course. I crawled back up to the course right away, but my goggles were full of snow, so I had to race the rest of the way without goggles; from there on I took the whole course straight, but I had already lost about 15 seconds in the fall. I ended up in 38th place with the time of 1:41:7.

Even with a bad fall, Gus was uninjured as the team stood in 4th place after Dartmouth, Denver Univ., and Western State College. As he approached the next event, Gus was not optimistic:

> Then came the ski jumping day, and I did not feel very good. We had a lot of altitude sickness among the team members, and I had a touch of that in the morning. I jumped late in the competition, and had a pretty good jump in the first round and had the longest jump; in the second jump I jumped too early and did not get the distance, but in my last jump (two out of three jumps) I hit with everything I had, and it ended in victory, American NCAA [National Collegiate Athletic Association] Championship, while Gunnar finished second.

As with everything in Gus's life, it seemed when the odds were against him, he came out on top. Gus was ecstatic after the event, and later that day the team celebrated.

> We drove down to Denver that evening after the award ceremony. As first prize I got a nice trophy, a nice pair of slalom skis plus merchandise worth about $ 40 - and that isn't bad!? In addition, I got a certificate for jumping, cross-country, and 4-way combined, where I finished 11th.

The team had a great flight back to Seattle, and the best prize was Claire waiting for Gus at the airport. School was looming ahead with many of the team a bit behind---including Gus—but with hard work he pushed ahead. His test in a CPA course yielded a perfect 100%. Math courses were also going splendidly. This was a good harbinger of what was ahead because he had to take the CPA exam in a month. It would be a grueling three-day test. Few pass it the first time around. All of this was in hopes of landing a good job for a bright future with Claire. "I have been downtown to talk to various bosses in firms about possibilities for a job next fall. I have been on top of the list in every firm, besides having good grades and good connections, and my name is in the papers once in a while. So there will be no problem getting a job one place or another."

Easter Sunday fell on April 9th that year, and Gus spent the holiday with the Thompson family. His letter home was full of plans and a preview of where he'd be married.

> Believe it or not I went to church with the family Easter Sunday!! It is actually the church I am going to be married in. It looks like I am going to get married around September-October, but there could be many changes before then. I figure on going up to Alaska again this summer to get some money in the bank before I get married, then get married and take a small trip, and come back to a job.

Chapter 23
Charging Ahead

By May 1950, Gus had a lot to report to his proud parents. He had managed to get all A's in all his courses in the last quarter of school; quite an achievement for a young man who, only few years prior, had to learn to speak fluent English. Besides great grades, he worked as an assistant to one of his professors. In his travels, he won the coveted NCAA ski jumping championship in Colorado. He and Claire were having a marvelous time together attending dances and dinners. Beyond that Gus wrote, "[I am] chairman in Beta Alpha Psi, and was named Honorary Captain of our Univ. ski team for 1950, have my picture hanging on the All- American wall in the large indoor stadium, got my name on the Honor roll for my grades." Quite a resume for a recent immigrant!

The marriage date shifted from October to August, while job possibilities were starting to solidify. Arthur Anderson, a giant in the world of CPA firms, was recruiting Gus. But Gus had second thoughts for good reason.

> They told me that they had cut the list way down, and that I was still on the list, and that they would like me to come down and talk with them some more etc. The next day I went down for the appointment, and the boss

spent about 1 1/2 [hours] with me in his office. We talked about everything there is about auditing etc., and at the end he said they were seriously considering me, and that they would like to hire me. At the beginning I was flattered that they had selected me over some 100 applicants, and he was very honest with me. He told me all about the job both advantages and disadvantages. I would say that if I was not going to get married this Fall I would have taken this job without blinking an eye, because it is the largest CPA firm in the USA. The reason I did not accept in the first round is that with this kind of job it means one would be out traveling all the time.

In the meantime, Gus had heard about a job in Wenatchee, a town of about 7,000 inhabitants about 200 Norwegian miles from Seattle. One of his professors had called to set Gus up with the head of personnel. This ability to network played out beautifully in Gus's favor:

They had many applicants, but today I was down to talk to the owner of the firm, since I was the one who had been recommended for the position. I have now been employed as Chief Accountant for Jim Wade, who owns 2 large companies and who is the largest apple grower on this side of Mississippi. He owns two corporations, one is the apple orchard operation where he employs 800 workers during the season, and then he has a corporation which has large warehouses and cold storage for his own fruit as well as for other fruit orchards. It is in the latter that I am employed as Chief Accountant. I have a beginning salary of $250 per month, and I was told that the increases come often and large, especially if it is a good season. In the warehouses we have room for over 300,000 boxes of fruit!!! My job consists of keeping track of the books, set up the results of the business, balance the accounts, income and loss accounts, set up income and expenses in the future, and keep track so we always have enough cash to handle the daily operations, as well to figure expenses from petty cash etc. Later it is great possibilities for promotion, since one of the bosses soon will move.

The other big attraction was the town itself. Gus described Wenatchee as…"a very cozy town, farming and fruit on grand scale, not like around Lillehammer." The weather was also a plus when it came to skiing. "It is cold in the winter and warm in the summer." In fact, it was close to Leavenworth where they had jumping hills. "…from 10 m to 85 m, where I can train. I am sure I will have some time to go skiing, because our season is during the summer and fall." But most of all it was perfect for his fiancée. "Claire is very excited about this, because she has always dreamed about living in a small town with a lot of fresh air, and not so much stress which Americans are known for."

Gus already knew some people in Wenatchee, and it was only a three hour drive to Seattle and Claire's family. According to Gus, the owner was not only a kind and decent man, but known throughout U.S. for his fruit business. The date of June 15th had been set to start the new job.

Beside the new job, there was more exciting news for Gus's family, "Claire and I are going to get married August, because then it is a little quiet in the office so I could take a few days off after the wedding." Also looming ahead was the CPA exam, and graduation. "The 10th of June Claire and I will be marching up on the podium in cap and gown to receive our graduation certificate for completed studies at the university. Then I move to Wenatchee right away to start to look around for an apartment for Claire and I."

On the lighter side, Gus needed to let his mother know the latest on his hair. "Mamma, I now have my hair parted on the side again, I let my hair grow out this spring, because I realized that I was going to have a little more respect with this." As it was, Gus didn't need a new haircut to garner respect. He'd already accomplished so much, and there was more on the horizon.

Chapter 24
June Was Busting Out All Over

June was a month of milestones for Gus and Claire. Both of them graduated from the University of Washington. Gus graduated debt free and with honors. Decades later, Gus had crystal clear memories of that day: "We were walking around in long gowns and a four cornered cap with tassel. It was in all 1,900 of us who each received our degree during a 3 hours solemn occasion at the University with speeches." What a moment that must have been; all that hard work had paid off. Gus had a degree and was on the threshold of a new career and marriage. Of course, Gus and Claire celebrated together.

> I then went home to Claire where I was over the weekend. We went horseback riding on two pretty good horses for about an hour. We galloped and had fun riding along trails in the woods. Afterwards we went to an aquarium with octopus, fish, seals, crabs, etc. Later we went to a movie. We were allowed to borrow Mrs. Thompson's car and drove to Seattle.

Soon after, it was time to kiss goodbye. Gus was off to Wenatchee to start his new job with J.M. Wade Fruit Company. Claire was on her way to Chicago, Washington, DC, New York, and Quebec. Once Gus was in Wenatchee, he realized it would be difficult to find a place where he could get reasonable room & board. Fortunately, he found a good option:

> I talked to my boss who turned out to be a very nice man. His name is Soucie (1/2 Norwegian 1/2 French). He took me with him to his home, and let me have the second floor in his home, where I have a very nice room, lots of closets for all my baggage. He gave me a small radio I could use, he and his wife asked me to feel completely at home there. I eat breakfast and dinner here, and lunch in town. I drive to and from the office in his 1950 DeSoto car.

The DeSoto make was founded by Walter Chrysler in 1928. It was named after a Spanish explorer, Hermando de Soto. After 2 million were built, by 1960, the model was discontinued. Gus must have enjoyed the size and style of the DeSoto, but along with an impressive car came some real challenges. "At the moment I am toiling with the books to get acquainted with the methods and procedures in the firm. And just as Gus was trying to get settled, his boss, J. M. Wade who owned four companies, asked Gus if he was interested in taking a job up at his apple orchard in Malotte, including all the accounting. This was initially a dilemma.

> Unfortunately, I am not really that interested, since the place is fairly isolated, with few people to be around, we don't have a car, so we can't go to town, no busses, we have no furniture etc. Claire would like to work and

do something, so she is not sitting at home and look at the walls, and also so we can save more money, to be able to take a trip to Norway soon. Wade said he would take care of the furniture, and arrange it so I could have a 1940 Plymouth car to use, but I don't think Claire would like it. Personally I would like it better to be here.

Gus was quickly finding out how lucrative the fruit business could be. He wrote, "In one month we collected over 7 million Kroner! Of course, almost as much is going out, but the money is changing hands in large quantities. Soon the cherries will be ripe, [so] it will be very busy. Last year we made $ 170,000 (12 million Kroner) on cherries alone, in addition we have pears, apples and apricots later in the fall." Gus met again with Mr. Wade, and realized there might be plenty of possibilities for him. "He said he wanted young vigor in the firm and teach them all they can learn. This sounded pretty promising, and that depends on [me], of course, but there are wonderful opportunities for me." Gus decided to take the Chief Accountant position that Wade offered in Omak which is nestled in the foothills of the Okanogan Highlands. He wrote to his parents:

> Therefore I am now up here at the apple orchard, which he also owns, it is another corporation. He wanted me to be here approx. 1 1/2 months, so I could see how life was here at the Orchard, and get the smell of the whole thing. I have been here a little over 2 weeks now, and like it OK. We are out riding horses almost every

> evening on the prairie; otherwise we are playing cards, go to movies, or go for a drive. We have approx. 20,000 apple trees here, so you can understand that this is a big operation. The downside with this whole thing is that there [is] hardly anybody to be together with around here, and nothing is going on here. There are only a few miles to the Canadian border. I am working with 9 other people in the office, and I do the most difficult part of the work here, since none of the other people have any extra education in the field. Arthur Wade (a nephew of Mr. Wade) and I live in the same house here, and are together quite a bit, he is 29 years old. We are going to work together in the future.

This area of the country was also giving a young man who grew up in Norway a real taste of Americana. This was cowboy country!

> Last Sunday several of us went to a cowboy town and watched a rodeo, where they had events to see who could ride the fastest after a calf, throw a lasso around the calf, jump off the horse, and tie three feet together, so the calf could not get up. The winner made it in 25 seconds! Another event was to ride wild horses with and without saddle, and the one who could sit on the horse the longest was the winner. They also had an event where they rode wild bulls and tried to stay on the longest, and finally an event where they rode a horse full speed after a bull, then jumped on the neck of the bull, and tried to twist the neck of the bull and get it to fall down with the feet in the air. The winner made it

in 8 seconds! This was all new to me, so I had a lot of fun.

While both Claire and Gus were busy that summer, her family had lots to do. "The Thompsons are now frantically preparing for the wedding, they are planning on about 400 guests, so I guess it will be a big deal, they are so sweet and kind." But there is a bittersweet note for Gus. "Two of their friends have offered to have a dinner before the wedding, a dinner which is normally hosted by the groom's parents." To take such a big step without his beloved parents tempered his excitement. "It is only so unbelievably sad that you cannot be present at the wedding, it is completely indescribable, but unfortunately, I have not yet found gold in Alaska, or won in the lottery, otherwise there is nothing more I would like to do than bring you over here by plane, so you could be present."

For Gus, though, he continues to assure his parents---especially his mother---that he's making the right choice. And that his future wife is also yearning to meet his parents as soon as possible.

> I found the world's nicest girl, you know and that counts for a lot. I am only looking forward to the day when I can afford to travel home on a trip with her, and be home for a while to visit and talk endlessly, [there] is so much that needs to be said. Claire and I are going to save like mad, so we can reach our first goal as soon as possible. You see she agrees with me that traveling to

Norway is [number] 1 on the program. I can understand that you are a little anxious because Claire is American and speaks American, and perhaps may have different ideas, and is used to different things than I am, but I can assure you that the only difference between Claire and I is that her parents are in USA and mine are in Norway. She is as you know, 22 years old now, is an excellent swimmer, plays tennis with me, goes skiing, sings, plays the piano, and is all in all a very sporty girl, something I must have. She has read a lot about Norway, and knows more about Ibsen, Bjornson, Grieg etc. and Norway's history than I do. She has also on her own purchased a beginner book in Norwegian, and I have helped her a little, but hope to have more time when we are married.

There was also urgency with timing of the wedding; Gus was in danger of being sent back to Norway. Even Gus's activities during the war needed to be verified. There was no way he would lose the love of his life. He and Claire were committed to move ahead for good reason.

Mamma is a little afraid that I am getting married so soon after I finished school, but that is almost a necessity unless I continue at the University, since my visa is only good if I attend the university. Therefore I need to get married before the University starts again in the fall. After I am married then I will apply for an emigration visa with Claire's help. In the meantime I need more documents from Norway, so I am going to ask Mamma to obtain an attest from Lillehammer Police about my position during the war, and one attest that I have never been arrested, that is all I need, and they must both be in English.

Again, there is closure in this letter. America will be Gus's home. "As you can understand I really thrive over here, and am planning to settle here permanently. It does not look very promising in Korea, but time will show what happens. You see I could get called into the American Armed Forces." Fortunately, Gus didn't go into the armed forces, but he was marching ahead to a very promising future.

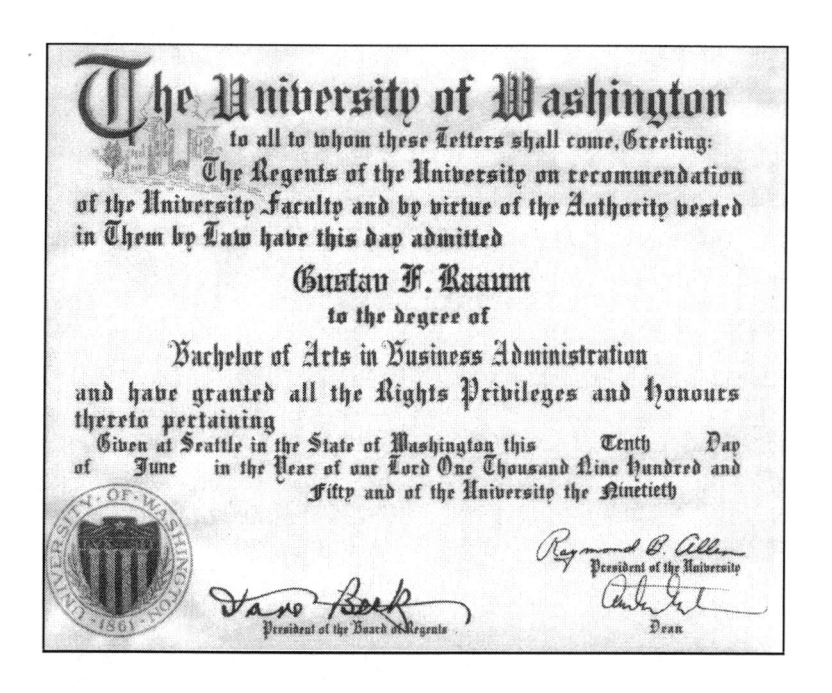

> **The University of Washington**
> to all to whom these Letters shall come, Greeting:
> The Regents of the University on recommendation of the University Faculty and by virtue of the Authority vested in Them by Law have this day admitted
> **Gustav F. Raaum**
> to the degree of
> **Bachelor of Arts in Business Administration**
> and have granted all the Rights Privileges and Honours thereto pertaining
> Given at Seattle in the State of Washington this Tenth Day of June in the Year of our Lord One Thousand Nine Hundred and Fifty and of the University the Ninetieth
>
> Raymond B. Allen, President of the University
> President of the Board of Regents
> Dean

Chapter 25
The Fruits Of Labor

Gus was toiling away in what he called "the desert" at the Johnny Appleseed Orchards in Malott, located within the greater Omak area. He was asked by his boss, Mr. Wade, to be there at least six weeks. His main concern was how Claire would feel about the place. Gus was, in fact, enjoying certain aspects of the area. "The first week I was here we went out horseback riding almost every evening. The horses belong to the boss here. I am truly a cowboy now." As with most men at that time, Gus became enamored with the cowboy lifestyle. "We have been to a rodeo where real cowboys competed with lasso, caught calves, rode bulls and wild horses etc. That was a great experience."

When he wasn't out on the range or at the rodeo, Gus was at the movies, out for a drive in the country, or singing in a small men's choir. He was never at a loss for something to do, and thankfully he had skiing to look forward to with a ski area located only twelve miles from home. The area also held a bounty of creatures. "Concerning wild life up here, there are lynx, rattlesnakes, deer, birds, bear etc., but they are not as dangerous as one might think."

Mr. Wade was very satisfied with Gus's work. He knew he'd hired a smart young man with a great work ethic. "He [Mr. Wade] said that he wanted to bring in young talent into the firm (like me), and give us the best training and then eventually turn the whole thing over to us. The whole thing sounds like a wonderful future for me in this firm. Time will show." But the most important person Gus needed to impress was Claire. Finally, his beloved came over for a visit, and got a taste of life in eastern Washington.

> Claire came home, and she came over to Wenatchee Saturday morning, so I took one of the cars and drove down to Wenatchee Friday evening. She came with her mother's car. We drove all round town to try to find an apartment for this fall, we saw a lot of places, from the worst to the best ($80-$90 a month for 4 rooms!!!). We then went to a baseball game and saw Tacoma play against Wenatchee, and Wenatchee won. It was fun. Claire rooted for Tacoma, while I rooted for Wenatchee.

Then Gus drove Claire north to high country. Their future would hinge on how Claire felt about Omak. "I took Claire with me to the ranch here, so she could see the whole thing, and decided that she would like to come for a year. It is always sunshine and is warm here. We went out riding last evening, and today I showed her around the orchard. Claire likes it so well that it is quite possible that we will be here a year." This was great news, and Gus's boss was eager to sweeten the deal. "Mr. Wade would very much like for me to be here, and they were going to arrange it so we get an electric stove, oil burning furnace, paint the inside any color we wanted, give us a car to use." That car was a 1946 Chevrolet. All of this persuasion worked. Claire and Gus had committed to their first place together. "We have also arranged for an apartment in Omak with living room, nice kitchen with refrigerator, electric stove, etc., bedroom, nice bathroom, washing machine, garage and it is only two blocks from the school where Claire possibly will get her job."

Claire returned to Tacoma where she would have several different wedding showers, i.e. a kitchen shower, a linen shower and so on. The wedding was coming up fast, and Gus had his part to do. "I am going to try to take a trip to Tacoma before the wedding to buy a wedding band, and get a marriage license, to see Claire and help a little with the preparations." Gus kept his parents informed as a way of keeping them included. "Claire and the others are very busy with the plans for the wedding. It looks like about 350 guests will be invited to the church and the reception afterwards." In addition to a piece of wedding cake he would send home, Gus also made another promise. "We plan to record the whole formality in the church on a phonograph record, so you can listen to it home in Norway." The wedding would take place at the First Lutheran Church in Tacoma. Gus and Claire had already chosen the place they would go for their honeymoon: Carmel-by-the-Sea.

Throughout this time, Gus was not only missing his parents, but he was still very concerned about his father. Because of his father's accident, there wasn't much they could do in the way of financial support. Gus must have sensed this, and wanted to make it very clear they had reared an independent son who loved them no matter what.

> Pappa, you don't have to worry about me, because I do not need any support or help of any kind; because with my health and education and still several hundred dollars in the bank, and married to the nicest girl in the world, I don't need any support. In addition, I feel so much better about the fact that I can stand on my own feet; I am very happy that you have supplied me with so much common sense; once in a while Claire tells me that I have too much common sense.

That common sense would be worth its weight in gold as far as Gus's professional life. And, as far as his choice for a wife...well, that was the *pot of gold* at the end of the rainbow.

Chapter 26
Yours Gustav 8/25/50

Gus & Claire's wedding day

The festivities began on Wednesday, August 23rd at the Thompson house. About twenty people were in attendance. To pay homage to Norway, the Thompsons served some Aquavit (Water of Life) which is a flavored spirit produced since the 15th century in Scandinavia. Sigurd and Ingeborg Raaum were not forgotten, Gus recalled, "They were toasting for everything on this Earth, after a *skaal* had been made for you at home." After the celebration, Gus and the "boys" headed out for a night of fun. The Norwegian men turned out to be made of hardier stock.

> We men traveled to Olav Ulland, where we had the bachelors' party in good Norwegian style. The three Americans who attended gave up around 1a.m., and from then on there were 10 Norwegians left, namely, Gunnar, Jan, Olav, Christian, Kjell, Ole Lie, Arne Ewald, Reidar Ulland and me, and we lasted until 2a.m. I was carried (apparently) to bed by cheering friends, but Gunnar took good care of me.

The wedding would take place Friday August 25, 1950 on a clear, warm evening. Gus wrote the following account of what he was doing just before the big event. Thank goodness his bride had no idea where he was.

> The wedding time was starting to approach, Gunnar and I sat in a small restaurant downtown and ate a little, then we suddenly realized that it was 7:15, and we were supposed to be dressed in a tuxedo and be at the church by 7:45! We paid in a hurry and rushed to the house where we were staying, shaved, washed, brushed teeth while we were sitting on the toilet, but we made it to church by 7:50 PM, so that was OK.

As Gus and Gunnar approached the First Lutheran church, they heard the organ playing a piece by Edvard Grieg, a famous Norwegian composer. Then they heard Claire's friend sing in a mellifluous voice a hymn called, "I Love Thee." As the wedding march began, Gus and Gunnar slipped in from the side door, and went directly to the front of the alter. The air was thick with the sweet scent of flowers and anticipation. First, Olav and Jan walked slowly toward the altar, and then veered to the right, and up the steps. They stood one behind the other. They were followed by Christian and Bob Ross. Gus watched as his beloved Claire approached the altar.

> Then came the bridesmaids two by two, and then swung to the left. Then came Gen (Claire's sister), right behind her came a three-year-old girl who threw small flowers in front of where Claire was going to walk. Then Claire and her daddy came down the aisle (I smiled like a light the whole time). They stopped where I was standing. We three, plus Gunnar and Gen, walked up toward the minister who stood behind the alter ring. He prayed, and we repeated the words. Papa Thompson stepped back, and I put the ring on Claire's finger. We kneel, pray, and then we are man and wife. We rushed out of the church followed by Gunnar and Gen, and then came the bridesmaids coupled with each usher. Dick went back to escort Mrs. Thompson. After that we went back to the church to have a bunch of pictures.

After the pictures were taken, Mr. & Mrs. Gustav Raaum headed to their lovely reception. This is how Gus described it to his parents:

Gunnar and Gen drove with us to Tacoma Tennis Club for the reception, which was very successful. They took some more pictures when Claire and I cut the cake etc. Claire's girlfriends sang a love song. Gunnar proposed a toast for us, and then my fraternity brothers sang our love song. Claire threw out the wedding bouquet. We went upstairs and changed into traveling clothes. We rushed down the stairs and out the front door, while the guests were throwing rice all over us. Gunnar was ready outside with Mrs. Thompson's car, and rushed away at full speed. In advance we had hidden my car six or seven blocks away, so we jumped into our car where we already had our luggage. We said a nice good-bye to Gunnar and took off.

The next day the happy couple headed to Lake Chelan. (They didn't have enough time to take a trip to Carmel by the Sea.) Chelan was a great choice, though, because they could simply swim, relax and enjoy the sun. Then it was on to Meadow Creek for a glorious three days. Not only was it fun, but, for Gus, it brought back memories of a place in Norway.

We rented a small motor boat every day and cruised around on the lake. We fished and did some sunning. We caught some nice trout which were fried for us for breakfast. We also went on a long trip to another lake where we saw a well-known high waterfall, otherwise looked at the very nice scenery. It reminded me about Jotunheimen near Gjende. We went on a long hike one day, and we played badminton, and played cards in the evening. Then we drove back to the coast to Long Beach in Washington where they have a 40 km long sandy beach. We rented a small house with living room, kitchen and bath. We stayed there 2 days, but the sun was shining so hard the whole time, so we had to leave before we got burned up. It was nice down there, huge waves which roll in over the sandy beach, really fun.

Gus & Claire on their honeymoon at Long Beach.

It was a truly relaxing and idyllic honeymoon. Once the happy couple was back in Tacoma they opened piles of presents. After a quick trip to the Thompson's summer place, they were on the road to Omak in a car stuffed with gifts. It took them several days before they felt settled in. Gus was already a handy husband. "I made two bookcases, one for the living room and one for the bedroom."

The Raaums settled happily into their new community; Claire even joined the choir as Gus sang her praises to his parents. "Claire is an excellent cook, and very clever in planning meals with lots of fruit and vegetables."

Throughout the next 62 years together, Gus and Claire never lost the love and loyalty that was the foundation of their marriage. As a sign of Gus's enduring love, he had this engraved on the inside of Claire's ring: Yours Gustav - 8/25/50. Together, they would build a successful marriage, a family and a truly abundant life.

Although Gus's immediate family couldn't be there at the wedding, these letters show they were there in spirit. These letters were read at the wedding by Gus's best man, Gunnar Sunde.

Dearest Gustav, our son, Dearest Claire:

Here come Mamma and Pappa, via Gunnar, to greet you on the absolutely biggest of your, hopefully many fold, important and good days! For a long time now, our warmest thoughts have been circling about you both, and we have tried to follow along as you went along and as the days approached the most happy one, and please, excuse us that we have been unable to help, but the thoughts have been in our mind. It is at important family events like this that the distances feel like twice as far, and that we today cannot personally be present and to see our children shine!, makes our hearts heavy, and gets our tears to run. At the same time we thank the Creator that you two, who love each other, now are being joined and are going to your own nest.

Thank you, dear daughter, that your love fell upon our son. We are so thankful for that, specially because we understand that you are such a loving person, and therefore will such a good and understanding person for him. We look sincerely to the time that we can hug you, and wish you welcome to our home.

Also you, dear Gustav, we will press our heart and thank you for the wonderful years we had with you at home. Thanks for all the happiness, and thanks for the fact that you have never disappointed us! You were a blessed child.

We know you will now transfer your abilities to your future home. In addition to those, I am sure the bridegroom's manners, devotion, and romance will also be as necessary as sun and rain. Should trials come, who can avoid those? Then you have only one place to turn, and that is to the one in whose house you today have promised each other to be true. Do not allow one day to be spoiled, as long as you can help it, because, remember it will never come back, and life is so short.

Today, we will in our thoughts, be present at the formal church wedding ceremony, and with the following arrangement which we know will be without question, be the most beautiful frame for a day full of experiences.

Then would the good Lord quiet the world's storm, which we are truly anxious over, so that the days and years to come will be bright and peaceful for both of you, and us all. This we wish with our whole soul. May the lucky star follow you always !!

Let us all join in: Congratulations, and we who know " Gid de lenge lenge leve maa" (May they live a long time)....... (...and this should be Claire and Gustav's Skaal- Hurrah " !!??)

Our heartiest regards and congratulations to Gustav's mother and father-in-law over there, to Claire's sister and Gustav's sister-in-law, and other family, girl friends and friends, (and a special greeting to the Norwegian friends !)

This letter was written by Dick Raaum, also for the wedding.

Dear Gustav, Dear Claire:

It is a little odd to think that you are getting married today, Gustav, without us hearing your answer: Yes I will! to the question by the pastor. The distance between Tacoma and Lillehammer is unfortunately so long that we cannot hear your's and Claire's voices. However, it exists something from here which is faster that rocket driven airplanes, namely our thoughts. They will participate in full, that I can guarantee both of you.

I said that it was odd to think that Gustav is getting married, and that expression I can expand on. Now I must first inform you that Gustav and I have not been much together the last 7 - 8 years because school and work have kept us in different places. However, I have never heard that Gustav was interested in girls. It was actually a surprise when I read in his letters about his fascination for you, Claire. When some of the boys talked about such and such a "super licorice", then Gustav responded by asking what ski wax worked best on such and such snow, how far the Ruud boys had jumped last Sunday, and what results could be reached in such and such jumping hill. That was during the Winter, and if it was Summertime, he was either going to the stadium to practice for pentathlon, or went up in the mountains to fish. You all have to agree with me that it is odd that he today has jumped a deciding and most graceful jump straight into marriage.

And you, Claire, has he asked (I hope nicely) if you will be his partner for the rest of your life? We have only seen you in pictures, and only heard you through letters, but one thing is for sure, and that is that you must be something special, extra exceptional. When Gustav has decided then you must be so, and then he must be thankful and be extra happy that you have answered Yes. Gustav has always been real and straight forward, and from the time we have been together I only have good memories. Therefore, I am sure, dear Claire, that you will not regret the answer you gave today. Then I hope it will not be too long before you come to Norway on a trip, so we can meet you both and get to know you, Claire, something we are really looking forward to.

We almost feel like we are hearing the wedding bells, and we join in the choir of congratulations. Britta and I are trying, despite the distance between us, to voice over the others as we lift our glass and wish you the best of luck with the day and the future.

Dick

Part III

Two For The Road

Chapter 27
Deportation Brewing

Gus and Claire had settled into life in Eastern Washington; singing in the choir, learning to cook and community involvement. But to say money was tight would be an understatement. They lived in a small apartment over a grocery store. Gus described their meager furnishings, "We had only a bridge table and 4 chairs and a radio." And because the apartment had no heater, Gus recalled, "In the winter, it was so cold that fresh fruit sitting near the kitchen window would freeze overnight." But beyond that, a chilly isolation was setting in. In a letter to his parents (October 10, 1950) Gus complained, "It is too dead here for us young people who like to meet a lot of people and have lots of friends." It's clear, the novelty of Omak was starting to fade for two new graduates who were used to the excitement of campus fun; dances, parties and holiday weekends. On the other hand, Gus was willing to meet his commitment. A big part of his disappointment was he was originally hired to work Wenatchee (pop. 15,000). Omak is sparsely populated and best known for the Omak Stampede, a giant rodeo that began in 1933. Claire and Gus were learning that they weren't cut out for the cowboy life.

As Gus was setting his sights on the CPA exam and his next career move, U.S. immigration was setting their sights on him. In the following letter he told his parents:

Believe it or not, I got a letter from the US Immigration department in Seattle, where they said that they understood that I no longer attended the University, and reminded me that I had to leave this country right away after I had completed the university, and asked me to inform them what arrangements I had made to leave the country by November 4!

Fortunately, Gus had a friend who was a "high official" at the immigration office in Seattle. His friend informed Gus that he had been in the country illegally since June when he graduated. Theoretically, he informed Gus that he could be under arrest. On a trip over to Seattle, Gus and Claire had papers filled out, and he was fingerprinted. Gus also had to get friends to fill out witness documents vouching for him. The next steps would be a formal court hearing where his papers would be admitted and Gus could make his case for staying in America. After that, the case would be sent to Washington, DC where it could be considered by Congress to be approved or rejected. There was one silver lining in the process. "The good thing is that all this time I am waiting (almost as much as one year) to get this emigration visa I cannot be called into the US Armed Forces."

This turned out to be a long and complicated process that would take a few years to resolve. In the following excerpt from Gus's recollections, he documents his perilous journey.

They sent me a "Warrant for Arrest of Alien" from the Department of Justice, United States of America, dated November 6, 1950, signed by John P. Boyd, District Director, and Seattle District. It said [Gustav Raaum] "has been found in the USA in violation of the immigration laws of USA, and is subject to be taken into custody and deported pursuant to the Immigration Act of May 26, 1924, in that he has remained in the USA after failing to maintain the exempt status of a student under which he was admitted".

It states further that "Authority has been granted to release under $500 bond or on own recognizance if satisfied he will appear when wanted for further proceedings". I then filed an application for suspension of deportation, and later received a request to appear at a hearing at the Seattle Immigration Office on Feb. 26, 1951, My case was processed in Seattle, approved and forwarded to the Central Office of Immigration & Naturalization in Washington, DC, where the case was approved on July 17, 1951, and an order to suspend my deportation and a recommendation that I be given a non-quota immigrant status was submitted to U.S. 82nd Congress. I received no official word regarding the progress of my case until June 30, 1953, almost two years later, after having corresponded with Representative Jack Westland in the U.S. Congress.

Upon frequent inquiries at the Seattle Immigration Office I was told that my case was more or less a routine matter and that it was running its course. During that time the US Ski Association tried to speed up my case since they wanted me to represent the U.S. in the 1952 Winter Olympics in Oslo, Norway.

Representative Westland found out that for some reason Congress had not acted upon my case, and they had failed to notify me, so I had to start the process to become a US citizen all over again. I filed a petition for a non-quota immigrant visa, and we traveled to Canada for me to obtain this visa, and to re-enter the US. At that time the law required me to be a resident for another three years before I would be eligible for US citizenship. I appealed for leniency on this matter. I went to classes at Edison Technical School in 1955 to learn about US Federal, State and Local matters. The Naturalization Questions were numerous, 139 for the Federal, 40 for the State, 20 for County and 20 for the City.

Several years of struggling through the immigration process wasn't an easy time for a young married man starting out in a new life, but Gus and Claire maintained an optimistic attitude. Gus continued to pursue the American Dream. Finally his patience and perseverance paid off. "I finally got my US citizenship at an official ceremony in Seattle in 1956, and my certificate was issued 1/14/57."

Form I-206
(Rev. 12-19-47)
U. S. DEPARTMENT OF JUSTICE
IMMIGRATION AND NATURALIZATION SERVICE

WARRANT
FOR ARREST OF ALIEN

United States of America
DEPARTMENT OF JUSTICE
XWASHINGTONXXX
Seattle, Washington

No. A-6597658

To CHIEF, INVESTIGATION SECTION, IMMIGRATION AND NATURALIZATION SERVICE, Seattle, Or to any Immigrant Inspector in the service of the United States. Washington

WHEREAS, from evidence submitted to me, it appears that the alien GUSTAV F. RAAUM who entered this country at Northport, Washington on the 8th day of January, 1950, has been found in the United States in violation of the immigration laws thereof, and is subject to be taken into custody and deported pursuant to the following provisions of law, and for the following reasons, to wit: The Immigration Act of May 26, 1924, as amended, in that he has remained in the United States after failing to maintain the exempt status of a student under which he was admitted.

I, by virtue of the power and authority vested in me by the laws of the United States, hereby command you to take into custody the said alien and grant him a hearing to enable him to show cause why he should not be deported in conformity with law. The expenses of detention, hereunder, if necessary, are authorized payable from the appropriation "Salaries and Expenses, Immigration and Naturalization Service, 1951 ." Authority has been granted to release under $500 bond or on own recognizance if satisfied he will appear when wanted for further proceedings.

For so doing, this shall be your sufficient warrant.
Witness my hand and seal this 6th day of November, 1950.

JOHN P. BOYD
District Director
Seattle District

The warrant for Gus's arrest in November, 1950.

Chapter 28
Big Steps & Baby Steps

Much to the disappointment of his boss, Gus left Johnny Appleseed Orchards in 1951. That summer he found himself working in Alaska again. It was always a treacherous undertaking, and even if Gus didn't know what he was doing, he'd find a way to do it. This is Gus's account of his last stint in the wilds of Alaska.

> I took the job as chief mate since it was better pay and I had been a deckhand on another boat several years earlier. However, my luck had it that the captain of the boat was a sourpuss Norwegian deep-sea captain who expected the chief mate to know as much as he did. Then I knew I was in trouble, but I needed the job badly so I tried to bluff my way through. When I reported to the boat he told me to load a 34 foot power cruiser from the dock on to the ship's deck and tie it down for the trip to Alaska (while he went up town for some supplies). Since I knew many of the people on the dock I scurried to get some help and finally got the cruiser lifted on board with a crane, and tied down. We eventually started through the locks and headed north to Alaska. He told me to take the first shift at the wheel. Needless to say, I was not too sure of myself, but I turned on the radio to cheer myself up, and I got out Hansen's handbook, which was the Bible of the sea. It showed bearings, distances, times to go from here to there, compass direction, navigation lights etc. Pretty

soon the Captain yelled up to me, Shut that God Damn radio off, I'm trying to get some sleep. I thought if the Captain knew how little I knew about navigation he would not sleep much. It was getting dark, so I kept checking the lighthouses, and after a while I got pretty good at it, since every lighthouse was identified. We finally arrived in Ketchikan at the cannery.

It was while sitting on the boat in Ketchikan that Gus received news that would direct the course of his career; after years of study, he finally passed the CPA exams. What a relief after all the work and effort he'd put in. But the immigration process and the military were looming on the horizon for Gus. After a few months in Alaska, he had to leave abruptly to register for the draft. (He surprised Claire after he landed out of the blue in Seattle.) Gus was informed that when his student status ended, he should have registered immediately. It was a very serious matter because he was one year overdue, and all of this could endanger his bid for U.S. citizenship. Once he registered, his hope was that as a married man, he would not be called up for service. Fortunately, that would be the case.

Now that Gus had earned his CPA status, he had to work for a CPA firm for two years to get his certification. His first "professional" job in Seattle was at a firm called McLaren, Goode, West Co. (One of the partners already knew Gus because he had gotten him the job at the orchard.) It turned out that Gus had had his eye on this firm for more than a year. He even mentioned in one of his letters home that he "…had yearned for this position for a long time." It was this kind of networking that would help Gus to climb the corporate ladder. This was quite a feeling of prestige, as he stepped into the real world of finance. "I was very happy to get that job, which required that I buy a hat and have some nice dress-up clothes." And just as he had hoped, the summer job earned him enough money to buy, "…a 4-door Plymouth sedan for about $1200." This was a huge accomplishment back in a time when a car was considered both a luxury and a necessity. Gus told his parents that their, "1949 Plymouth Special Deluxe, four-door, with radio and heater, dim lights and white sidewall tires was dark blue like the Norwegian flag." Clearly, he was very proud of this purchase!

Of course, this was also a time for the Raaums to make a new home. They found it at the brand new Northgate apartments in Seattle. This is how Gus described it to his parents:

> We have a balcony, nice bedroom, living room, modern kitchen with refrigerator and electric stove, very nice bathroom with shower and bathtub etc. The washing machine and automatic dryer, and storage are in the basement. The walls are in very light green with white ceiling. The building has just been completed and has 8 apartments, and the building is one of numerous such buildings which are part of a huge project. Directly across the street is a huge, hyper modern shopping

center which consists of 90 different stores which sell everything between Heaven and Earth. The buildings which are brand new are located in the outskirts of Seattle, and an express bus goes to town every 20 minutes. The whole thing is fantastic. We move in September 1st, and we have already been looking around for furniture. One sofa costs $ 200.00 !!!!!, but it lasts a lifetime, a low table in front of the sofa, one high back arm chair for me, a beautiful heavy little table for a lamp and pictures, and rugs. This evening we are going out to look for a bookcase, a bed with mattress, and a chest of drawers. It's kind of nice to walk around with my wife and look at furniture, prices etc. I am so happy that I came down here so early, so I can take part in buying for and planning our future home.

Now that there was a new job, and a new home, it wasn't long before there was a new baby. While living at the Northgate apartments, David Lindsay Raaum was born on June 8, 1952. Gus recalled, "That happy event changed our life considerably. Dave had quite a bit of colic which kept all 3 of us up quite a bit of time, and walking the floors. The one bedroom apartment became too small."

Even though it was too small, Gus and Claire welcomed his brother Dick who emigrated in February of 1952. Dick had traveled from Norway on the S. S. Stavangerfjord, the same ship Gus had worked on many years before. Dick slept on an army cot for a few weeks before securing a job at Jantzen Knitting Mills in Portland, Oregon. As was the case with his brother, Dick was not afraid of hard work. He started out sweeping the factory floors to eventually managing the entire factory.

Both Gus and Dick would one day fulfill the dream of the financial success in their new homeland.

Gus & brother Dick are reunited at King Street Station, Seattle.

Chapter 29
Life Begins And Ends

Claire, Gus & David at their Densmore home.

After living in a one-bedroom apartment for a time, Claire and Gus were thrilled to become first-time home buyers. They moved to a house in North Seattle on 137th and Densmore. (That little house still stands today.) For every young family in America, this was the goal… home ownership. This was how Gus described it in his memoirs:

It was a two-bedroom home with one car garage, living/ dining L-shaped room, kitchen and one bathroom, with floor furnace. I made shutters for the windows and we also put in grass in the back yard, which was full of rocks, which we cleared out. We were very proud of our new home. We paid $9,750 for this house. We did not have enough money for the down payment, so we borrowed $2,000 from Claire's dad, and paid him back promptly.

Throughout their marriage, Claire's family was always supportive, and that was especially appreciated when it came to buying their first home. Gus commuted to his job while Claire worked as a full-time Mom. Her job duties doubled with the arrival of Christian Erik, born on March 11, 1954, coming in at a hefty 9 lbs. 8oz. A few months prior, Gus's parents had emigrated. They arrived in New York on January 25th on the same ship Dick traveled on, the S.S. Stavangerfjord. With Sigurd and Ingeborg also living in their small house, it became quite crowded. Fortunately, some kind neighbors, Mario and Mary Peila, offered their spare room to the Raaum grandparents.

It would be good to report that Gus's parent's immigration had a happy ending, but it did not. Sigurd was a proud man who wanted to find work, but at the age of 58 it was difficult. Also, he had suffered a traumatic head injury while in Norway. He'd spent many months recovering from a fall, but the aftermath had left him feeling

Sigurd & Ingeborg Raaum at home in Lillehammer, circa 1948.

depressed. (Gus noted in his memoirs that Sigurd had a setback on the voyage over, but didn't elaborate) When his son, Dick, found him a retail job in Portland, Sigurd left his wife behind to start the job and eventually find a place for them to live. Dick had asked his father to stay with him, but instead he went to the Benson Hotel. There is still no clear answer as to what happened on that summer day in 1954, but the newspaper reported that Sigurd Raaum plunged nine stories to his death. One hypothesis was that he was standing by the open window, and was overcome with a dizzy spell. But his family suspected otherwise; they believed it was suicide.

Dick received a call that day from a Portland detective telling him, "His father was in an accident." When Dick asked how he was, the detective replied, "He's dead." As Dick recalled this event more than 60 years later, he was still visibly shaken. He was asked to come down and identify his father's body. What a horrific ending for a son who only wanted to help his father find a new beginning. What made matters even worse, was Gus and Ingeborg were in transit to Portland when it happened. Dick was tasked with having to tell his brother and his mother their loving father and her husband was gone forever. Sigurd's ashes would be sent to the land he had loved and left, Norway.

The family was devastated, especially Ingeborg. At sixty-one, she was not only bereft of her beloved husband in a strange country; she didn't speak English, was indigent and had never worked outside of her home. But Gus stepped up and helped his mother find a place to live and a profession. He found her a large house to rent in the University District which was converted into a home for the elderly and bedridden individuals. Ingeborg received her license to be a caregiver, and was quite successful at her new profession. Gus would help with house repairs, and pick his mother up every Friday at Pike Place Market where she did her shopping. He also did the bookkeeping and assisted with paying bills. Claire was also a great support; she and Ingeborg got along well and shared a deep love and respect for each other. Ingeborg retired at the age of sixty-four and eventually moved into a small apartment.

During this time, Gus was climbing the corporate ladder. His company had merged with a large international firm, Haskins & Sells. Gus recalled, "We had a great staff at the firm." The only downside was it took him out-of-town a lot, "…which was tough on my wife, but great for my experience." On one of his audits, he was sent to a Wenatchee automobile agency where he discovered the office manager was stealing money from the firm. In Gus's words, "His wife was a big spender."

In 1955, Gus had the opportunity to work for a new company started by Frank DeBruyn, an employee of Isaacson Iron Works. The company was called Pacific American Commercial Company (PACO). Gus quit his CPA firm and became the new controller for PACO which evolved into a world class construction equipment supplier. This is how Gus described his job:

> I had to set up the books and records of the company, organize the office, hire a secretary, get telephone service, etc. The company dealt in Army/Navy surplus from all kinds of unused tools, drills, and all kinds of used equipment from winches, to dragline buckets, pumps, compressors, cranes etc. We used an old warehouse building on the waterfront North of Spokane Street. The same building housed Allied Tractor Equipment Co., which had the same owners; they fabricated bulldozer attachments, and scrapers. We went to auctions and bid on government surplus sales. I

worked for PACO for some 10 years, then I transferred to Allied Tractor, and in the 12th year I transferred to Young Corp. which was owned by Bob Lindberg and Hank Isaacson.

Throughout this time, Gus was active in the Washington Society of CPAs, the Seattle Ski Club, Pacific Northwest Ski Association, US Ski Association and FIS (aka the International Ski Federation). Life at home, in the corporate and sports world was good. The future was opening up with new opportunities.

Chapter 30
Always An Adventure

By 1955, another house was on the horizon. The family moved to what was called "Mom's dream home" in Blue Ridge. The charming colonial had even been featured in a national magazine. This time their growing family had three bedrooms, and plenty of room to grow. Even though Gus was able to sell their last house for what it cost, he would still need to borrow to buy the new one. The cost was about $20,000, and he borrowed $3,000 from a close friend. As always, Gus paid back the loan quickly. He noted that they were able to move all their old appliances into the new house. In the following description, Gus describes how well they settled into their new neighborhood.

> We were very active in the Blue Ridge Community Club. I served on the Board and became President of the club in 1961, when we built a new clubhouse and swimming pool. We were also active in the Magnolia Presbyterian Church where I served on the Session and was also chairman of the big annual fund drive. I became an Elder in 1961. We were also active in the Scouts, since our two sons were in Boy Scouts of America. I served as a Cub master in 1961.

The house was a joy from the beginning. Gus and Claire put a lot of hard work into it. "We painted and added many features. We also enclosed the porch and made a den out of it. With the help of neighbor Bob Wolter, I replaced the kitchen counter, and added a dishwasher." Gus was also improving on his career by joining the Washington Society of CPAs and the American Institute of CPAs.

Gus with Dave & Chris at Blue Ridge.

The next big addition was their third child, Lisbeth Ann, born on March 11, 1960. Gus and Claire were thrilled to add a girl to the family. He proudly wrote, "Having a daughter really completed our family, and the fact that she was born on Chris' birthday made it double fun." Gus added that this became triple duty for Claire, "…but she loved being a mom. Her degree at UW was in nursery school specialty, so that came in handy with our own family." The children attended Crown Hill grade school and the boys went on to Whitman Jr. High.

Even with a very full family and professional life, Gus kept up with his participation in the skiing world; serving as the Board of Directors for the Seattle Ski Club and the US Ski Association. He was frequently the Master of Ceremonies at the USSA and the PNSA conventions and related banquets. And, of course, he promoted ski jumping in the Northwest as one of the founders of a club called "Kongsbergers." According to the club history, it was originally created by a "hearty group of Norwegian skiers." Gus's good friend, Olav Ulland, was head of it. At the time, there was a small run and a warming hut. Today, the club still exists, but there's no more ski jumping; the last meet was in 1974. The club now focuses on cross-country skiing.

In 1965, Gus organized a special summer ski jumping tournament as part of the Nordic Festival on August 22nd. This proved to be an engineering feat based on hay, ice and grit.

> The ski jump was built by pipe and clamp construction (Patent Scaffolding Co.) starting on top of the Coliseum roof (by Wick Construction) and Rainier Ice Co. supplied approx. 40 tons of ice which was crushed into

spring snow. 230 bales of hay were used to cover the plywood decking, and chicken wire was used to hold the hay in place. Fire dept. was concerned about the straw and all the people (12,000 spectators). There was a rodeo in the Coliseum at that time, so we were afraid the horses would eat the hay. Both Dave and Chris jumped on this hill off the Coliseum roof.

The ski jump at the Seattle Coliseum, 1965.

As the sons of a Norwegian and American ski champion, there was no way either of them could have avoided performing this amazing stunt. Chris was only 11 when he made that jump, and more than 50 years later he can recall he was "shaking" as he made that plunge.

The following event that Gus organized shows when he made a decision---by hook or crook ---he'd make it happen. His description of the following event seems to show he could actually move a mountain…indoors!

> Another time the Junior Chamber of Commerce organized a ski festival in the Civic Ice Arena. Dan Evans was President of the Chamber, and I was asked to help organize a jumping tournament inside the arena. To get enough in-run, we had to open a hole in the brick wall in one end of the arena. Outside we had scaffolding all the way up from the ground and we built the in-run up and out far enough to get some speed before the take-off which was inside in the ice arena. We applied crushed ice on the plywood platform and applied chemicals to keep the snow from melting. We had a nice jumping competition, and Olav Ulland also made several summersaults off the take-off, and his skis barely cleared the rafters of the roof structure. Spectators enjoyed the show.

Winter and summer activities were always fun, and engrained in the children. "We took the children up skiing. We went to Snoqualmie Pass most of the time, sometimes to White Pass, Stevens Pass, Mt. Pilchuck, and Crystal Mountain." Between 1963 and 1966, Gus ran a ski jumping school for Seattle area kids at Crystal Mountain. The school featured a 20 meter and 40 meter hill. Both Chris and Dave attended the classes and jumped every weekend during the winter months. In addition to frequent camping trips, the family spent the month of August at the Thompson vacation home on Vashon Island. During the week, Gus commuted to the island ferry terminal, parked his car and jumped on the ferry to Seattle. Being on the water held all kinds of fun: "We bought a small sail boat, a Sea Scouter, which we used quite a bit. We had all five us in the boat. We also bought a small speedboat, from Walt Hampton in Wenatchee. It had twin 18 HP outboard motors on it, and we did some water-skiing behind it." Gus and Claire shared a loved for the sea and boating their entire married life.

Those were twelve wonderful years living at the Blue Ridge house and all that Washington State offered, but a wonderful opportunity would take the Raaum family on a whole new adventure. They would leave the Great Northwest for another---equally spectacular--- part of the United States.

The Grand Tetons.

Chapter 31
Jackson Hole - The Next Frontier

As Gus relates in the following passage, life was more than good in Seattle---it was idyllic. But an offer he initially refused grew more attractive as he took a good, hard look. For Gus, everything he did included the Big Picture; whether he was leaving his homeland or working in Alaska. It was always about how he could move ahead in life. And Jackson Hole would be the next step on the ladder to success.

In 1967, I got a call from Paul McCollister, who was the President and one of the owners of Jackson Hole Ski Corp, in Jackson Hole, Wyoming. Graham Anderson had recommended me to him. They were looking for a new manager of the Ski Corporation. Gordon Wren was the first manager there, but he was being replaced. At that time I had a nice job, we had a nice home in Blue Ridge, and access to a nice summer place on Vashon, we both had our widowed mothers nearby and many nice friends. So at first I turned him down. He kept after me, and finally our whole family took a camping trip to Jackson Hole to take a look. We stayed at Paul McCollister's log home ranch out on Antelope Flats. Paul showed us around and his wife Esther was most hospitable. We discussed this situation as a family and I decided to take the job. I thought it would be a chance for me to be in charge of a company and it would help me grow in my professional life, and it could be financially rewarding if all went well, and it would be a nice experience for our family to move from a big metropolitan area to a small town of some 2,000 people in a healthy climate.

Another incentive was talk of having their children bussed away from their regular schools in Seattle to other areas of the city. As with most parents, Claire and Gus wanted to keep their children in neighborhood schools. But the biggest incentive was a new annual

The Raaum family at the Alpenhof, soon after moving to Jackson, 1967.

salary of $25,000 plus 2% of the net income of the company. Gus negotiated a good deal, and quit his job. Because he was such a valuable employee, though, there were no hard feelings; in fact he left with money and a promise. "The Isaacson's gave me a check for $ 3,000 as a thank you for a job well done, and told me I had a job any time I wanted to return."

After finding a renter for their Seattle house, and a farewell party at the Blue Ridge clubhouse, the Raaums began a whole new chapter in Jackson Hole, Wyoming. It was a big change after living in their dream home with a neighborhood and community they had grown to love. As Gus recalled, the first big challenge was finding a place to live. "We ended up renting a house on Moose Street, the only rental available. It was a small house with three bedrooms and a basement." Now that they had two boys and a girl, Dave's desire to have his own room would have him living underground. "Dave ended up sleeping in the basement, and his room was made up of packing boxes for walls."

The children entered the Jackson school system, and the boys became involved in sports and scouts. Because Chris began to tower over his fellow scouts, he decided to drop out of scouts; however, he did reach the Life Scout award. Brother Dave traveled all the way to Seattle to receive his Eagle Scout award.

When Gus started his job at the Jackson Hole Ski Corporation in Teton Village, he had very little knowledge of lift operations, ski patrol and avalanche problems. His background was primarily in finance, operations and personnel. It would take him a whole season to familiarize himself with all the operations and manpower needed to run the company. Gus's main focus was to trim the payroll, run an efficient operation and establish confidence with the banks by cleaning up the balance sheets. This turned out to be a herculean task.

> I did not realize how bad the financial condition of the company was until I got into the operation. The owners, Paul McCollister, Alex Morley and King Curtis had to be convinced to convert the interest bearing notes to stock to reduce the liabilities of the company, and the interest costs. We went to the State of Wyoming to obtain low interest loans with long maturity, and other financing to infuse additional funds into the company. We were successful in obtaining the loans. Eventually I was able to convince Felix Buckenroth, President of Jackson State Bank, to give the company a $50,000 line of credit. Business people in the town of Jackson were concerned that we would "steal" a lot of business from the town merchants as we expanded the operation in Teton Village. It really turned out to be the other way, since the winter operation at Teton Village helped develop year around business for everyone in the area.

Gus rose to that challenge, but he quickly realized one of the biggest problems was getting the skiers by plane into Jackson during the winter. They worked with Frontier Airlines to improve service, however, the landing strip needed to be lengthened to accommodate larger aircraft. That meant getting the permits from the Park Service. The locals weren't happy about that idea, and fought the extension.

Another big challenge was getting summer tourists over to Teton Village to tap into some of the three million people who visited Grand Teton National Park during the warmer months. Gus recounted, "We ran a cable car all summer to the top of Rendezvous Peak for sightseeing and hiking. In addition, we offered horseback rides from the village."

As Gus forged ahead in Jackson Hole, he would face some formidable obstacles, but like everything else, he leaned in and took it on. A crucial and painful task was cutting back on a substantial amount of employees, and still be able to keep the company afloat. He trimmed back the payroll from 180 to approximately 90 people. In the following account, Gus describes the travail this created.

> This created a lot of hard feelings and unhappy people, but my job was to save the company from going bankrupt. At one point the ski patrol started to create some kind of mutiny. I told them that we could either use all the patrolmen full time at one-half pay or we could use one-half of the patrolmen at full pay. They opted to all work at one-half pay. It was clear that we had too many people on the payroll, and it was my job to determine how we could run the company with fewer people. Some employees were not qualified for the job they had, so we had to make painful decisions to let employees go. That is one of the most difficult parts of being in charge of a company.

Beyond cutting staff, to increase cash flow it was decided they should sell lifetime lift passes. This created immediate cash, and Gus noted, "Those who selected this would later find out how smart they were." Then Gus attempted to go after the big guns:

> During this time we tried to find major investors for the company. I obtained an appointment with Mr. DuPont at his office in Florida. His office had high security, but he said the investment was too far away for him to be involved. Later I obtained an appointment with Lawrence Tisch of Lowe's Corp in New York City. He was a skier and had hotels and other investments. We were only looking for a couple of million dollars, and his response was that he did not want to be involved so far away for so little money. So we struck out twice.

Since the resort operated seven days a week and on holidays, that was also Gus's schedule. He was very grateful to have a wife who enjoyed the challenges of rearing the children, a lot of the time on her own. He also had "…a very dedicated ski staff." But the job continued to have challenges. "To bring in extra cash, the stockholders went through a stock sale registration to obtain additional cash for the long-term capital investments necessary to expand. This stock sale was not very successful." But there were bright spots, "The company sold lots and condominiums, which created revenue." Those sales of real estate bolstered the net income of the corporation and kept the company alive.

Along with that kind of growth would be the impact on tapping into resources. "We had to increase the sewer plant which was under the permit process of the County. After a long process we succeeded in being able to increase the capacity. We also had to secure adequate water supply for the resort." Mother Nature continued to be in charge of progress. They needed to clear more land for ski runs, and that meant reducing boulders to smaller rocks. But blowing things up came with an inherent risk.

> One day, in the fall of 1969, we had a very serious accident while using dynamite. One large rock flew high up in the air and hit the main cable for the aerial tramway. This rendered the cable car inoperative for a period of time. We had to hire cable experts to come in to inspect the damage, and determine, to the satisfaction of the US Forest Service, whether it was safe to operate the tram. We had some very anxious moments, but it turned out OK. We could have faced replacing the whole cable, and risk losing a whole winter season without the use of the tram.

Jackson Hole wasn't all work and no play. In fact, it was the home of the one and only "Gus Raaum's Original Amateur Hour" performed at the Pink Garter Theater. As the newspaper wrote, "There was no age, residence or educational requirements; no discrimination on basis of race, creed, sex or athletic prowess." That meant the Raaum children could also perform. Lou Ann appeared in a brown polka-dot dress, and sang until her own father "gonged" her. The next indignity was her brother, Chris, used a fish net to pull her off stage. Chris and his two friends performed in giant hats which obscured half their bodies. Each had a face painted on their stomachs which moved in rhythm as they whistled the theme from the movie, "Bridge on the River Kwai." The production was staged by the Jackson Hole Ski Club and profits were used for alpine and junior racing programs. A good time was had by all, and decades later, is still fondly remembered.

Off stage, the Raaum family grew to love that area of the country, and took full advantage of it. Everyone in the family, including Claire, was a talented athlete and enjoyed the great outdoors.

Gus Raaum's Original Amateur Hour

Chapter 32
The Sky's The Limit

Jackson Hole is nestled in one of the most spectacular places in the world. The Grand Tetons' jagged peaks rise above pristine lakes, amazing wildlife: moose, bison, elk and bear, and the Snake River. Life in Jackson Hole offered incredible outdoor activities for the Raaum family. On Gus's limited time off, he learned how to fly fish in spectacular rivers and lakes. Wyoming was also a mecca for miles of scenic hiking trails. For Gus, having grown up in Norway, the mountains and water must have brought back marvelous memories of his youth. That love of the outdoors always stayed with him, and left an indelible mark on his wife and children. At that time, the Raaum family couldn't have picked a more beautiful area to live.

But nature was not without its dangers. One incident shook the family to its core. On a beautiful winter evening, Gus, Claire and a few friends took a snowmobile trek. It was an enjoyable night among friends until Claire's snowmobile plunged off a bridge into a frozen creek. She landed with the machine on top of her. It was a harrowing accident in the middle of nowhere. Somehow, they located a door to place her on and carried her back to the car. She was rushed to Jackson Hospital where it was determined she had broken six ribs and had a punctured lung. Claire spent many weeks in the hospital, and when she was released her dear mother, Rhea, went to Jackson Hole to help care for her and the children. Fortunately, Claire recovered completely, and throughout the rest her life she was able to ski and swim and keep physically fit.

Aside from the great outdoors, the family joined many community activities; they became members of the Baptist Church where Claire sang in the choir---occasionally as a soloist. Gus was a member of the Jackson Hole Ski Club and the Jackson Hole Rotary Club. He started as the Rotary secretary, and was later voted to serve as president.

The newly built house at Teton Village, Wyoming.

A great opportunity opened up when Gus was able to purchase a residential lot at Teton Village for $8,000. Next step, he and Claire decided to build a home. A contract for $45,000 was signed, and construction started in the fall of 1969. Gus and his builder, Don Schuch, scoured the countryside for rocks to build a magnificent fireplace. Gus called it, "Our dream house with many special things built into the house." It turned out, Mr. Schuch came in under budget, and returned several hundred dollars to Gus upon completion---something that's unheard of today. The family moved in the spring of 1970.

Jackson Hole was often crawling with high-profile people. Gus recalled, "When the Governor, Stan Hathaway, came to ski I spent time on the slopes with him. When other VIPs and close friends came to visit I did take a few runs with them." In January of 1969, Gus and Claire met Robert Goulet and his wife at a function at Jackson Lake Lodge. Warner Brothers came to shoot a spy film called *Mrs. Pollifax Spy* starring Rosalind Russell, and rented the tram for five days. Gus recalled that Russell did not enjoy floating above the slopes. "The actress was deathly afraid of heights, so she sat on the floor of the tram on the way up." This turned out to be a great opportunity for Chris too. "Chris worked for the movie company several days and made a lot of money."

There were lots of opportunities for socializing in Jackson Hole. Gus remembered one particular occasion that started on a positive note, but didn't end that way: "We had in our home a big cocktail party for a lot of VIPs from Frontier Airlines, but we were shocked to learn later that Frontier cut back on their flights into Jackson." That was also a bad year for snow. In fact, they had to cancel the USSA training camp for lack of snow. A Colorado company was hired to seed the clouds in hope of producing snow. In December, John-Claude Killy arrived and received a tremendous amount of publicity. Killy was a French World Cup alpine ski racer who dominated the sport in the late 1960's. He was a triple Olympic champion, winning three alpine events at the 1968 Winter Olympics. Killy also won the first two World Cup titles in 1967 and 1968. Fortunately for Killy, and everyone else, snow arrived on December 22nd, and the chair lifts were opened.

Life was a blur of travel and activities. In January of 1969, Gus traveled to Europe for the Federation of International Skiing (FIS). When he returned, he organized the National Ski Week at Jackson Hole ski area. In February, Dave and Chris raced in alpine competitions at Pine Basin. For his daughter, Gus acted as the master of ceremonies at a Girl Scout banquet that March. Then in May, he was off to Barcelona for the FIS Congress. "I stopped over in Lisbon, Portugal overnight and toured Lisbon the next day. It was such a nice place I sure wanted to go back there sometime and spend more time."

Travel---around the world or around the United States--- would become a big part of Gus's career. "I traveled to Stratton Mountain, VT to attend the National Ski Areas Association annual convention. I made a talk to the Grand Teton National Park employees about summer and winter recreation activities. I attended meetings of the Intermountain Ski Area Assn. on many occasions at Park City and Sun Valley."

During Gus's last year at Teton Village, things were about to change again for the Raaum family. In the following excerpt from Gus's journal, he describes how the journey to Montana began.

> I was contacted by a headhunting firm, Struggles and Struggles, who was looking for a President for Vail Resort in Colorado. At the same time I was contacted by Chrysler Corporation which was looking for someone to head up the anticipated development of Big Sky in Montana. At that time being President of Vail Resorts was probably considered the plum job in the whole country in that industry. I took a hard look at it. Our family went to Vail for a visit, and to meet with Pete Seibert (then President), Bob Parker (marketing manager) and several members of the Board of Directors. I told them that I would think about it. I told Pete Seibert that if my job was to be a hatchet-man and bring the financially troubled company to profitability, then it would difficult for me if he was around Vail and unhappy employees would run behind my back and

complain to him etc. There were three finalists for the job of President of Vail, me included. Pete Seibert called me later and said that if I would take the job, he would move to Denver. We looked at the school system near Vail, and it looks like we would need to put our kids in school in Denver, living away from home. This we did not like. In addition, being President of Vail would require a tremendous personal commitment with cocktail parties and other functions when VIPs came to the resort. This would leave very little time for the family. I finally on June 8, 1970 wrote Pete Seibert and told him to withdraw my name as a candidate. The interesting thing was that the other two candidates also turned the job down. If I had not had the offer to be in charge of Big Sky at that time, I would have been very tempted to take the job in Vail.

Big Sky, Montana was now on the horizon. This would prove to be a marvelous and extremely challenging time in Gus's career. But the same Viking spirit that brought him to America and had taken him this far…would carry him on to the next challenge.

Chapter 33
Big Sky Country

Gus didn't intend to be president of the Big Sky Resort, in fact, he didn't even apply for the job. Because his reputation preceded him, he was one of seven resort managers who were *invited* to interview for the position. Gloria Chadwick who was the executive director of the U.S. Ski Association recommended Gus for the job. The Chrysler Realty Corporation was sponsoring the development of Big Sky, so Gus flew to their headquarters in Detroit to meet with their top executives. This trip was done under wraps. "I tried to keep the trip to Detroit secret, since I did not want the employees and owners of Jackson Hole Ski Corporation to know that I was looking at other jobs." After Gus returned home, he was contacted by Ed Homer, President of Chrysler Realty, who wanted Gus to bring Claire with him to Montana to meet TV news giant, Chet Huntley and his wife, Tippy.

Chet Huntley was best known as half of the Huntley-Brinkley Report on the NBC networks that began in 1956 and lasted for 14 years. Chet had a special spot in his heart for Montana because he was born there in the tiny town of Cardwell on December 10, 1911. After a long and illustrious career in broadcasting, Chet returned to Montana in 1970 where he wanted to build a ski resort called "Big Sky" south of Bozeman. It would be a massive job that needed the right people to make it happen. Gus clearly recalled the trip he and Claire made to a small motel that stood at the entrance to what would become Big Sky.

> We drove up on May 31st and met Chet and Tippy Huntley. We got along very well, and that was important to Chrysler, since Chet was to be the Chairman of the Board, and I was to be President and CEO. We clicked right away. The next thing I knew I was offered the job, which I accepted. An employment contract was prepared and executed. Initial salary was $40,000 per year increased to $45,000. Later I received a $20,000 bonus.

That was the good news; the bad news was announcing his departure from Jackson Hole. Initially, his boss, Paul McCollister was deeply disappointed, but he quickly realized this was an offer Gus couldn't refuse.

> Paul wished me the best, and we had a great relationship after I left Jackson Hole. I knew that Paul needed me to continue at Jackson Hole Ski Corp., so I felt badly leaving, but I felt good about having saved the company, and made every effort during my 3 years to make the company successful. As soon as the employees heard that I was leaving for Big Sky many of them came to me and wanted to come with me to Big Sky and work for me there. Fortunately I did not need many employees at that time, and I did not want to rob Jackson Hole Ski Corporation of employees they

needed to run the company. I drove up to Bozeman on June 17th to attend a board meeting of Big Sky, and the Board at that time officially hired me and elected me President and CEO of Big Sky.

The Raaum family would have to leave their new house in Teton Village where they had lived only two months. Claire stayed behind with the children until they had finished school. Gus left for Montana and stayed at the Lone Mountain Ranch. On August 22, 1970 the Jackson Hole house was packed up, and Claire and the children headed for Bozeman. Their eldest, Dave, had graduated from Jackson-Wilson High School and was accepted to the University of Wyoming. The house in Teton Village sold quickly. "We sold our home in Teton Village in less than a week for $75,000 and we were very pleased with that, since it cost us only $53,000. In later years we heard that our house was on the market for $895,000."

When Gus started his new job, he was sure of his abilities. And because only one employee at that time came from his previous employment, he had to build everything from scratch.

> I arrived at Big Sky with a lot of confidence. At that time I was of the opinion that I could run any company in the USA. Since I was the first employee I had to build the staff from scratch. Lynne Poindexter, who worked for Jackson Hole Ski Corp. agreed to come up

to Big Sky to be my executive secretary. Other than that, all employees we hired were new to me.

The house Claire and Gus purchased in Bozeman would be their home the entire time they lived in Montana. Chris and Lou Ann went to local schools, and eventually they both graduated from Montana State University with degrees in film and television. Throughout those years, Gus commuted daily from Bozeman to Big Sky. In the wintertime, it was a very treacherous trip on a two-lane road through Gallatin Canyon. Gus endured the danger to make sure he honored his number one commitment: family. In the following excerpt, he describes what this was like.

> I elected to commute to Big Sky daily, not only so the kids could go to Bozeman schools, but also I did not want to have a close personal relationship with people who worked closely with me at Big Sky. When we moved the offices to the Mountain Village I had a 104-mile round trip commute. I left home early in the morning, often while it was still dark, and I returned home after dark in the evening. I worked almost 7 days a week on a regular basis, and did not take much time for vacation.

Claire embraced her life as a full-time mother. She was very involved in every aspect of the children's lives. The children remember their father being gone a lot. With the creation of Big Sky resort, in addition to his long commute, Gus had taken on a herculean challenge. Big Sky had the distinction of being the first and newest major destination in the state.

> It was a huge project, which started with planning, then into construction, and into operations as the facilities came on line for use and occupancy. Some of this was all going on at the same time. It was difficult to get the right people in the right jobs when we needed them, and to let them go as we had to meet other requirements, and they were no longer needed. It was difficult to find people with the proper experience who were willing to take the job in a somewhat isolated area of USA. We often interviewed the potential employee and his wife at the same time, to make sure they would survive in our environment. The Big Sky project had a lot of notoriety and we attracted thousands of unsolicited employee applications. Chrysler Realty Corporation, who was the majority stockholder, provided a lot of support personnel throughout the initial organization and during the growth of Big Sky. Most of them were great men and they did a fine job with enthusiasm.

There were some major bumps in the road when it came to personnel. Gus fired two people who were in powerful positions. Both complained to Chrysler's top brass, but Gus survived the onslaught. He was smart enough to alert Chrysler executives ahead of time, and they trusted his judgement. As time went on he built a great team. "We had a lot of wonderful and dedicated people working with me at Big Sky. Most of them were willing to do whatever had to be done when it needed to be done." With tremendous challenges ahead, that can-do attitude would prove to be the measure of success.

Overseeing the construction of the triple chair.

Chapter 34
Mountains Of Challenge

Long before US Highway 191 was paved, the route leading to Big Sky was an Indian and wildlife thoroughfare. It was a treacherous path that was crisscrossed with steep grades and several fords of the Gallatin River. So it was a momentous time in the spring of 1970, when construction for Meadow Village began and the official Big Sky logo was created. The following October, the ground-breaking ceremony for Meadow Village took place. That summer, Arnold Palmer arrived to assess the land for a golf course that he would design. Turned out, building a golf course in the wilds of Montana posed some big problems. For instance, cattle were breaking through fences, and trampling newly seeded fairways; deer were eating the leaves off of the trees. Some problems were manmade---workers had brewed a fertilizer that was too strong and proceeded to burn up the new grass. The golf course was finally finished in July of 1974. Beyond the golf course, during the entire process of building the resort, Gus recalled that Big Sky was plagued with legal and financial challenges:

> Since Big Sky was the first and newest major destination resort in Montana, we had to plow a lot of new ground. At the same time the college-based environmental armada was very active in the early days, trying to do everything they could to harass and

delay our project at every turn. This kept our legal department busy and our planning up in the air for some time. The delays cost Big Sky a lot of money.

Chet, Arnold Palmer and Gus (far right).

Securing the name of the resort was also another hurdle. But as a famous newsman and the Chairman of the company, Chet Huntley knew how to get things done. Fortunately, Governor Forest Anderson embraced the development; however, the name would pose a challenge. Gus recalled how the name "Big Sky" was granted.

On August 4th, 1969 Chet Huntley and Ed Homer went to Helena to visit Governor Anderson. At that time Chet said to the Governor, "I'll spend the rest of my life working on this project if you give me just one thing." The Governor replied, "If it is in my power you've got it." Chet said, "Give me the name of Big Sky for this project." Anderson picked up the phone and called Secretary of State Frank Murray and told him, "For the first time we are going to give the name Big Sky to a corporation, Big Sky of Montana." Later, Governor Anderson told Chet, "Hell, I thought you were going to ask me for the whole State, and I would have been hard pressed to say no."

Big Sky was Chet Huntley's dream, and because of his position in the world it gave the project a very high profile. But there was also an unexpected snafu because Chet was also known for his liberal views. The resort had applied for federal designation of the road spur from the main Gallatin Canyon road to the Mountain Village. They would need Federal Highway funds, but a major roadblock developed.

On September 10th, 1970 we received a telephone call from Ott Tschaache saying that the White House was mad at Chet Huntley for his derogatory comments about President Nixon in Life Magazine, that our application for Federal Funds to construct the highway spur to the Mountain Village was in trouble, the application was being held up. He made reference to Tom Lias, assistant to Harry Dent who again was the assistant to the President. Suddenly our many months of working with numerous State and Federal folks to achieve a highway spur to our Mountain Village went up in flames. Even Chet Huntley's calls to Senator Mansfield's office did not unclog this problem.

Eventually, access to Mountain Village was accomplished, Gus stated, "Big Sky built the road, but it was later redone and paved by Montana Highway Dept. The first 3 miles were done in 1977 and the upper 6 miles in 1979."

Beyond getting the highway planned and executed, there were massive challenges in other areas, including environmental groups. Like playing a game of whack-a-mole, it seemed every time one problem was solved another one popped up. Gus was constantly on high alert:

> Big Sky followed closely the progress in the land exchange negotiations between the US Forest Service and Burlington Northern, since Big Sky's development would be heavily affected by which way it would go. Environmental groups sued Big Sky. In their effort to delay or stop their progress, these efforts cost Big Sky several million dollars in holding costs and timing, but did not change their detailed plans, which were carefully developed with the environment in mind. Big Sky, of all people, had the most to lose if they did not take good care of the environment.

Communications was another hurdle. Big Sky's phone system was an eight-party line. By todays' standards, they employed a primitive way to handle the problem. Gus recalled, "When they needed temporary telephone service to the Mountain Village for early communications, they hired a helicopter to roll out a telephone line from highway 191 to the Mountain Village, about 10 miles, and they laid the line on top of the trees. Hungry rodents gave them a challenge to maintain reasonable connections."

When a new system was put in, Big Sky was assigned the 995 exchange. Chet Huntley would make the first *royal* call. Gus fondly remembered the event. "He placed a long distance call to the Queen of England, but the Royal Palace declined to accept the call, so Chet Huntley ended up talking to NBC's main correspondent in London." That was Chet Huntley's way…think big.

According to Gus, after an "enormous construction period" Big Sky opened for skiing on December 15, 1973. Governor Tom Judge was among the first to take a ride on the new gondola. At that time, a lift ticket was $7.50 and it gave access to all runs and lifts. Big Sky had a triple chair lift; the Andesite chair lift and the Explorer lift for beginners. Bethlehem Steel supplied the eight miles of wire rope needed to complete the massive project. But along with the success of opening the lifts, there were more fires to put out. Gus said, "The Mountain Mall was not completely finished, there were roof leaks and other things like delayed installation of kitchen equipment, carpeting, floor tiles and completion of the lower gondola building, but it was open for business."

Everything that needed to be done took tremendous effort, even getting enough electricity. According to Gus, 1974-75 was particularly tough because Big Sky's power supply had only *one* single power line. Even bringing in the New Year posed a challenge:

> On one New Year's Eve, with some 3,000 guests on the property, the power went out. Huntley Lodge was full of guests. The hotel staff quickly brought out lighted candles. The chefs fired up all the barbecues available, and Huntley Lodge offered free champagne. The guests were very patient and ended up enjoying the unusual evening with a late dinner. But a bigger concern was about frozen pipes, since the temperature was way below zero and Big Sky had all electric heat.

During the time Gus spent at Big Sky, he clearly faced enormous challenges. But what's truly amazing is to realize all the other responsibilities and activities he was involved in. He somehow managed his full time job and a growing family with the following positions:

> I was a Director of American Land Development Assn.,
> I was chairman of the Big Sky Home Owner Assn. (i.e.

mayor of Big Sky), I served as Chairman of the Architectural Committee, as Big Sky's first Postmaster, was founder and first President of Big Sky Ski Club, served on the Board of Rural Improvement District (sewer district), and was Chairman of the Board of Lone Mountain Springs, water utility, I was ski consultant for US President's Commission on Olympic Sports, I was member of Private Industry Advisory Committee to the Bureau of Outdoor Recreation, Dept. of the Interior, and I was chairman of the Resort Advisory Council of American Land Development Assn. I also served as member of the Technical Advisory Council- water quality preservation management planning for Madison and Gallatin River drainages, Southwestern Montana. Those positions were held at different times and for different periods.

Beyond his family, faith and his work, there would always be a precious place in Gus's heart for his homeland. The history of only a few Norwegians in America began as early as 1630's, but the organized immigration really began in 1825. This group came to America seeking religious freedom. Several dozen Norwegians set sail from Stavanger, and made a 14 week journey to land in New York harbor. So, to celebrate his Norwegian heritage, Gus kept the history alive and well in Montana.

In January 1975, I was a founder of the Fjelldal Lodge of the Sons of Norway in Bozeman. On the 17th of May that year we held our first celebration and I made a short speech in Norwegian. "It is a pleasure for me to honor the 17th of May here in Bozeman on occasion of this gathering of Norwegians and their family. Fjelldal Lodge of Sons of Norway was established at the beginning of this year, and this is the largest undertaking to date. Some 500 people came to see, hear music and taste Norwegian cookies. Thank you to all whom helped to bring personal things to exhibit, those of you who baked cookies, and those of you who worked to set this all up. This year it is 150 years since Norwegians emigrants landed in America on an organized basis."

During the eight years Gus would spend at Big Sky, he continued to face enormous challenges. One of the most difficult ones would be the loss of his colleague, and good friend, Chet Huntley. Together, they worked shoulder-to-shoulder to carve out a destination resort in the unforgiving Wild West. Sadly, only one of them would see the final fruits of all that labor.

Lone Mountain towers over the Triple Chair at Big Sky Resort.

Chapter 35
Chet & Gus

For millions of Americans, Chet Huntley was a TV icon. For Gus Raaum, Chet Huntley was a dear friend and business partner. On July 31, 1970, when Chet said his final goodbye to TV news, he told David Brinkley, "Good luck David, and goodnight for NBC news." Brinkley mentioned in his farewell that NBC had given Chet a horse as a going away gift. (The horse was named Julian Goodman, after former president of NBC and creator of the Huntley-Brinkley Report.) It seemed as if Chet was going to literally ride off into the sunset toward Montana. This next and final chapter of his life would be rich with adventure. But first, about that horse…

Gus's daughter, Lou Ann, recalled it was a Tennessee Walking Horse, a gaited breed that's known for its four-beat running–walk and flashy movement. It was originally developed in the south and used on farms and plantations. These elegant animals were a natural for the show ring, but according to Lou Ann, not the best choice for Big Sky country. Lou Ann remembered the stallion was shipped across the country, swaddled in blankets. And because it was a stallion, she described him as 'hot" as in *spirited*. Chet allowed Lou Ann to ride him, but the horse was eventually gelded to make him more manageable.

Chet was not only born in Montana, but he would go back over the years to vacation there. In the 60's he would visit the West Fork and Lone Mountain several times. The original idea for Big Sky came to him in 1968, while on vacation with his wife, Tippy. Chet started to inquire about buying some recreational lands that could be developed into a resort. By February of 1970, the backing had been secured and Chet was elected chairman of the Big Sky board. Initially, Jean-Claude Killy was invited to ski Lone Mountain by helicopter, and gave the thumbs-up. There was a possibility the French skier would become more involved with the resort, but that was the beginning and end of Killy's interest.

That July, Gus arrived and was named President and CEO of Big Sky Montana. The following October, a ground breaking ceremony was held for Meadow Village. Various recreational activities were planned, among them, snowmobiles. Gus and Chet got along famously, but they disagreed on the use of snowmobiles. Chet wanted snowmobiles to be part of the ranch operation; however, Gus didn't think it was a good idea. To convince Chet, Gus took him to West Yellowstone to watch snowmobile races. After experiencing the noise and the smell of exhaust fumes, much to Gus's delight, Chet agreed. There would be no snowmobiles on the ranch!

Ironically, even though Big Sky would have fabulous golfing and skiing, Chet did not ski or play golf. As some who knew him said,

Gus and Chet on a trail ride at Big Sky.

"He simply loved being there." The natural beauty in the area of the country was unsurpassed. Chet's love for the outdoors included fly fishing and horseback riding. Mike Foley, who worked closely with Chet, recalled a funny incident when a visitor stopped by the office on Highway 191. He asked the receptionist if Chet Huntley was just a name they used for publicity, and did he actually go there? The receptionist asked if he'd like to meet Chet? After he said yes, she pointed to the man mowing the lawn as Chet Huntley, and told him to go on out and say hello.

Chet and Gus worked tirelessly to promote Big Sky, whether it was getting road signs erected by the Montana Highway Department or traveling throughout the state speaking to numerous clubs and organizations about Big Sky and its plans. According to Gus, "Over the first two years we each made about 75 speeches. Chet also spoke at large national conventions i.e. American Medical Assn., and the like, which gave enormous exposure for Big Sky." Gloria Chadwick, Vice President and Marketing Director, also worked with them to encourage growth. She arranged for the US Olympic Cross Country Team to train at Big Sky. She organized the Big Sky Winter Carnival which included dogsled races. In fact, Chet and Gloria named most of the ski runs: Killefer was named after Tom Killefer, the Chrysler manager. (It was eventually changed to Mr. K in honor of the late Everett Kircher, founder of Boyne USA, later the parent company of Big Sky.) "Tippy's Tumble" was named for Chet's beloved wife.

Chet embraced his new life in the beauty and clean air of the state where he was born. But a deadly habit would cut his life short. Chet came out of the culture of a newsroom; a place of high tension fraught with breaking stories and deadlines. Chet was a chain smoker like many other famous journalists at the time, including Edward R. Murrow. He continued to smoke even after he left the business.

In the fall of 1973, after a long horseback ride with Gus Raaum and others into Beehive Basin, Chet Huntley complained to them about a pain in his back that didn't go away. He went to see a few doctors on the east coast. They thought the pain was spine related, so they put him in traction in the hospital. In early January 1974, Chet wrote a letter to a doctor in Seattle, who wanted Chet to speak to a group, in which Chet stated: "At the moment I find myself in the hospital with some sort of back and hip ailment, and there are indications that it is going to take a considerable amount of therapy to get me back on my feet." Unbeknownst to Chet and his doctors, it was lung cancer.

In the meantime, J. Walter Thompson Co. had prepared a detailed advertising plan for Big Sky to be launched in early spring of 1974. The plan had 8 different mailings to be sent at carefully timed dates and intervals. It included a 45-RPM record with a message from Chet Huntley, and other referrals to Chet. The advertising campaign was in the final stages when Big Sky learned that Chet had terminal cancer. According to Gus, even with a dire prognosis, Chet continued on. "The whole advertising plan had to be reworked, since its release was planned for dates subsequent to Chet Huntley's anticipated death. Chet tried chemotherapy, but had a terrible reaction to this drug and did not want any more treatment. He assured the staff that he was going to beat it."

Chet died shortly after at home on March 20, 1974 in the presence of his loving wife, Tippy. Ironically, it was only a few days before his dream was about to become a reality. Gus describes that time. "The Grand Opening of Big Sky, which was set for March 22-24, 1974, in fact became a dedication and memorial for Chet

Huntley with all the flags flying at half-staff. He had been very excited about the grand opening. He wanted to know whom he could invite among his many well-known friends. He mentioned Johnny Carson and others, but I felt that Chet Huntley was all that was needed."

After Chet's death, Gus took over much of the off-site activities undertaken previously by Chet. According to Gus, "The job was extremely difficult and required long hours, constant follow-up, and lots of supervision. The project needed extra cash investment by stockholders to carry the project through this difficult period, and the stockholders stepped up to the plate." On April 3, 1974, Big Sky welcomed Vern Blakley, on loan from Chrysler Realty, to become VP-Administration to specifically look after much of the on-site operations. Mr. Blakley was previously managing Director of Chrysler Corporation's operations in South Africa. He ended up as President of the company and Gus took over Chet's position as Chairman of the Board. In mid-June of that year, Big Sky was visited by Chrysler Corporation's President John Riccardo and his family. Below is a list that Gus compiled of what was onsite at the time:

> Big Sky had built or under construction 452 condominiums and 410 lots of which 303 condos and 288 lots were sold or reserved. Big Sky had 4 lifts, a 4 passenger gondola traveling 8668 feet, rising 1,525 vertical feet handling 1,150 skier per hour; the Lone

Peak triple chairlift traveling 3,036 feet, rising 833 vertical feet handling 1,800 skiers per hour; Andesite double chairlift, traveling 4,790 feet, rising 1,163 vertical feet handling 1,200 skier per hour; and the Explorer double chairlift traveling 3,745 feet rising 622 vertical feet handling 1,200 skiers per hour. The 1973/74 skier days totaled about 60,000. In addition to all the condominiums, the Mountain Hostel had 88 rooms (352 beds). The ranch had 16 cabins with accommodations for 45. The RV Park had 170 campsites. The 204 room Huntley Lodge was under construction anticipating completion in the late fall of 1974.

Chet Huntley's untimely death seemed to be a harbinger for the resort, along with other events that were forming a perfect storm. There were big changes on the horizon that Gus described this way:

> During this period of developing Big Sky, Chrysler Corporation had major financial problems and many analysts expected them to go bankrupt. This affected Big Sky, and we were faced with having to pull back on all fronts, lay off people, and operate with a skeleton crew. This set us back for a while. Then came the oil embargo, high interest rates, lack of mortgage money, and the mess with Nixon in the White House, several strikes by Montana unions, and our own Chet Huntley died. All of these factors were beyond our control, but had major negative effect on Big Sky's progress and timing.

Beyond all the changes that would take place, Gus looked to the future with his past as his foundation for success. And a big part of his past would always be Chet Huntley. In the end he remembered his friend this way: "Chet Huntley was a great man to work with. He was a very humble man with a great amount of wonderful stories to tell, places he had been and famous people he had met and interviewed." Chet Huntley's memory would forever be woven into the history and the dream of Big Sky.

Chapter 36
Goodbye Big Sky

The years that Gus spent at Bozeman were wonderful outside of the resort business too. The family was thriving and so were Gus's accolades. In 1971, Gus won the Julius Blegen Award, the highest award from the US Ski Association for his contribution to the sport of skiing. Gus was also listed in the Who's Who in the West, an authoritative biographical source that names movers and shakers. In the following excerpt, Gus lists some of his more personal accomplishments.

> In the early 1970s I helped coach ski jumping to kids in Bozeman. We built a small jumping hill east of town, near the cemetery. The hill was built with bales of hay. I also gave away all my large trophies to the Bozeman Ski Club, so they could use them for future competition. All they had to do was to change the label on the trophies. I also gave my jumping skis, which I won Holmenkollen with, to a local promising ski jumper. In 1974 Governor Tom Judge appointed me to the Federation of Rocky Mountain States' Travel Promotion Committee of the Market Development Council. On April 4th, 1972 Claire and I were invited by CONOCO to fly on their private plane to Banders, Texas where we stayed at the CONOCO private lodge

> over a long weekend, we flew back to Bozeman on April 7th. Chris graduated from high school on June 5, 1972. On June 6-8 I traveled to Sun Valley to take part in the NSAA annual convention.

But as time moved forward, Big Sky changed in a Big Way. Eventually, the Chrysler Corporation started to divest itself of real estate investments including shopping centers, student housing and resorts. One of the resorts they wanted to sell was Big Sky. Gus said, "I was not part of these discussions. They got hooked up with Everett Kircher who owned Boyne Mountain and Boyne Highlands in Michigan." In 1976, after a long period of negotiations, Kircher purchased Big Sky's operations and facilities, excluding lots, condominiums and acreage. For Gus, this was not what he had hoped for. "I ended up being chairman of the Board of Big Sky of Montana Realty Corp., a company that was formed to hold all such remaining real estate. I did not want to be President and CEO of that company since I did not feel qualified to market lots and condominiums." For Gus, feeling "unqualified" left him in a vulnerable position. And as he noted in his memoirs, more changes just exacerbated the situation.

> They brought in David Chamorro as President and CEO; he lasted 5 months and quit, because the Stockholders decided to sell all the real estate left in one package to Everett Kircher in 1977. I agreed to stay one year to assist in the

transfer of all the information and background information and be available for clarification. During that last year I did very little, Kircher's people seldom ever asked me about anything.

Big Sky had lost its luster for Gus, so throughout 1977, he started to look for other opportunities. One place was the Aspen Skiing Corporation who was expanding and building a new resort, however, that didn't go anywhere. Then, he considered the Disney Corporation who was planning a new resort in Mineral King, located in Sequoia National Park in California. Gus felt he had the right stuff for the position. "My 11 years in the resort business would be of immense value to a company trying to do the same thing from scratch, which I had just spent 8 years working on." But as Gus recalled Claire's reaction brought him down to reality. "However, my wife said, 'you are 52 years old, do you want to move to a small mountain town again and do this all over again?' She was not very anxious to make such a move." As it turned out, Claire was right; the Disney resort never even came to fruition because it was blocked by environmentalists. Gus continued to look for prospects in Montana, but it was not to be. As he recalled, "There really were not any opportunities, so we decided to head back to Seattle.

On June 18, 1978, Gus officially resigned from Big Sky. It had been quite a ride for him and his family. He and Chet Huntley left behind a legacy that has expanded and grown over the decades. Today, this premier resort is a popular summer destination, and in winter is known for giving skiers access to more skiing than any place in the U.S. Chet Huntley didn't get to see how far it had come, but Gus was able to return many times to visit. When the opportunity presents itself, David, Chris and Lou Ann still ski the magnificent trails of Big Sky. It stands as a monument to hard work, perseverance and the memory of their father who was always ready for the next mountain to climb…or ski.

Dave, Lou Ann & Chris skiing at Big Sky, March 2017.

Chapter 37
Hello Seattle

The next mountain in Gus's life would be looming over the beautiful city of Seattle, Mount Rainier. Gus headed for Seattle and stayed with his son, Chris who was working as a videographer for KOMO TV, an ABC network affiliate. Gus had a few leads; one was a newly developed resort in Lake Chelan, east of the mountains. Another offer was a position with part ownership in an insurance brokerage firm. Fortunately, neither panned out; there was a golden opportunity that came through a friend.

Gus left Chris, and he stayed a few days with long-time friends, Harold and Mary Fran Hill. After Gus told his friends about his job hunting quest, Harold said, "When you are through running around talking to all these people, let me show you what I am doing, and see if you are interested." As it was, Harold's investment company was swamped with work, and he couldn't even take a vacation. He also needed someone he could trust to talk about numerous lucrative projects and prospects. Harold believed Gus would make a perfect business partner.

Gus, not one to make hasty decisions, needed to sleep on the offer. "I thought it over a few days, and made a list of positives and negatives in various situations, and on May 17th, 1978 I decided to join

Harold. We agreed that we would try this arrangement for one year, and if it did not work out, we would shake hands, and each go our own way." They never did go their own way. Not only did the men form a deep and lasting business relationship…it would be the best professional decision of his life. Gus remembered how it unfolded:

> We formed Hill-Raaum Investment Co., a partnership, 1/1/79, which we operated on a 50-50 basis. The advantage for me was that Harold was already established, had banking connections, and had been in the business for many years in the area. I was the detail man, and Harold was the architect/engineer/contractor. It turned out to be a wonderful and successful relationship without a disagreement or misunderstanding in over 25 years.

A few days after Gus's decision to join Harold, he and Claire bought a house in Redmond (where they would live 18 years) and drove back to Bozeman the next day. "Our family packed up our stuff in Bozeman and sold the house there for $109,000." Lou Ann graduated from high school on June 1st, and the family left Bozeman two weeks later. Gus began work with Harold officially on June 19.

The first job done by Hill-Raaum was Northwest Food Brokers with Bud Ness. It was a small office warehouse building in Renton. They got the OK to proceed from Bud Ness on August 10, 1978. The project paid off, they made $ 50,000 on that project. The company turned around and used the money as a down payment on the nine acres south of NW Food Brokers in Kent.

Hill-Raaum started out on a roll, and has risen from there; buying, selling and renting commercial properties throughout the Puget Sound region. (Now Hill Investment Co., the company continues to thrive.) Gus was very grateful for the financial abundance which allowed him to provide well for his family in all kinds of ways. Whether it was vacations or educational opportunities for his grandchildren, Gus was incredibly generous.

Gus & partner Harold Hill on the job.

So many wonderful things happened through those years. Lou Ann attended Stephens College, but eventually transferred to Montana State University, like her brother, Chris. They both earned degrees in Film and Television. Chris was working as a shooter for a KOMO show called "Exploration Northwest" which had him traveling to places like Alaska, and beyond. Gus became a member of the Rotary Club on Mercer Island. Claire was back singing in the church choir. Their son, Dave, married Georgia on May 17, 1980 in Sugar Pine, California, the day before the eruption of Mt. St. Helens.

Throughout the years, Gus traveled extensively; most of the time it revolved around important sporting events. Gus describes one of his many trips:

> In 1979 I was invited to Sapporo in February to be Technical Delegate for their big international ski jumping competition, when I also held seminars for teaching Japanese ski jumping officials. I stayed in the hotel owned by Yoshiro Ito. There the staff greeted me "Welcome back Mr. Raaum". I was treated like royalty. When I wanted laundry done, it was done in 1 hour. Every day I came in to the hotel the front desk man had the key to my room when I came to the counter. They had a car and driver available 24 hours a day. He would take me to the jumping hill, and wait there for me with the motor running to make sure the car was nice and warm. Mr. Ito had a nice party for international

officials at his home. His home was sitting on a full city block in downtown Sapporo.

The following month, Gus found himself in Yugoslavia to act as Chief Measurer in the World Ski Flying Championships. The next month he was in Nice, France to attend the FIS Congress as a US delegate, and as chairman of the FIS ski jumping committee. Mixed in with international travel was a trip to Colorado Springs attending the US Ski Association's annual convention.

With all of Gus's involvement in the world of skiing, it's no surprise that the family had the treat of a lifetime: the 1980 XIII Winter Olympics. Gus was part of the planning committee for the games being held that year in Lake Placid, New York. "I made trips to Lake Placid in 1978 and also in 1979 to run the international ski jumping competitions in preparation for the 1980 Olympics. I traveled to Lake Placid in early February, 1980 to run the Olympic Jumping Competition." As part of Gus's agreement to do this, he requested that his whole family needed to be included. They stayed in a house rented by the Lake Placid Organizing Committee. It turned out to truly be a family affair:

Chris and Lou Ann worked at the outrun to check all suits used by jumpers to make sure they had the proper approval stamp. Dave manned the access to the judges stand to make sure only people approved for access got in, and Claire served hot coffee etc. to officials and VIPs, including Crown Prince Harald of Norway, Terry Bradshaw and Jamie Farr.

The Raaum family at the 1980 Winter Olympics.

The games were an absolute thrill for the entire family. The most memorable event was when the US Hockey team beat the heavily favored Russian team and Finland to win the gold. It became known in the US press as the "Miracle on Ice." As an added bonus, after the games, Claire and Gus flew to Ishpeming, Michigan for Gus's induction into the U.S. National Ski Hall of Fame.

Gus had the opportunity to fly off to Switzerland to chair the FIS jumping committee meetings where 34 from 14 countries attended. While in Europe, he got the royal treatment. "I met the President of Iceland, and King Gustav and Queen Silvia of Sweden in connection with Scandinavia Today program at Nordic Heritage Museum."

There was a sad event, though, in the following year when Gus's mother died at Totem Lake Hospital. She lived to the age of 86. Gus was always an attentive and dutiful son. He would show up each week to take Ingeborg shopping at Pike Place Market, her favorite place. In between, he would be at her place frequently to check in and fix anything that needed repair in her apartment. They had had a long and loving relationship, and she was greatly missed.

As always, Gus never forgot his Norwegian roots. He began meeting with a man named Svein Gilje to see about leasing the Webster School in Ballard to start the Nordic Heritage Museum. Gus became the first treasurer and one of the first board members when it opened in 1980. In October of '83, he met Norwegian Princess Astrid who visiting the museum. What a thrill! Still vibrant today, the museum serves as a gathering place to celebrate Nordic culture and art.

In that same year, 1980, Gus and Claire had the opportunity to go back to where Gus had spent a good deal of his youthful years... Alaska. As with all his trips to the last frontier, this one was also filled with adventure.

> In August we flew to Juneau, Alaska to join Hank and Carol Isaacson on their 65 foot yacht High Seas. On the way to meet us in Juneau, Hank had hit a submerged log and bent the propeller and shaft, so he was tied at the dock in Juneau. He was having Isaacson Iron Works in Seattle make a new shaft, and obtain a new propeller and have them shipped to Juneau. He had difficulty finding a yard able to lift his yacht to remove damaged shaft. He finally hired Manson Construction 400 ton floating crane to lift the yacht, but in lifting the yacht the deck started to crack, so they had to make some spreader bars, and then was able to lift the yacht up on the downtown dock. We had to climb down a long ladder to get off the ship, since we slept on the boat the first day, and had to use a Sani-can on the dock. We finally moved into a hotel in Juneau.

It wasn't long, though, before Gus and Claire were globetrotting again:

> In the Fall of 1980 we traveled to Europe, starting with London (where we visited Scott and Nancy Raaum), and then up to Scotland, later flew to Norway inspected Holmenkollen in preparation for the 1982 World

Championships, then we visited Raaum Farm in Fluberg, where my Great Grandfather and his family worked and lived. Then we traveled to Frankfurt, Germany to attend FIS Jumping Committee meetings. Claire and Siri Yggeseth had a chance to visit Heidelberg. We were gone 3 weeks.

Gus logged thousands of frequent flier miles by himself. The following February, he was in Steamboat Springs to officiate at the US National Ski Jumping Championships. Then, he was off to Norway to follow-up on Norway's preparation of the World Nordic Ski Championships. He spent ten days there for a "dress rehearsal" for the next year's World Championships. Then he and Claire were in the air again. "Claire and I left for Canary Islands to attend the FIS Congress there. Subsequently we visited Madrid and had a nice guiding and dinner in Madrid hosted by HK Aspirant Angel Baranda from Madrid."

During this time, Chris became engaged to the love of his life, Joanie. They married on January 30, 1982. The following June, Lou Ann graduated with honors from Montana State. Her reward was a one-month trip to Europe where she visited several countries. Lou Ann returned to Helena, Montana and got a job at a TV station.

At the beginning of May, 1983, Claire and Gus took off on another big adventure. Their entire marriage they traveled together.

They clearly had a passion for travel and each other. This trip down under it would be another unforgettable journey.

> We traveled to New Zealand, rented a car and traveled all through the Northern Island, fished in Lake Taupo, had a great trip, met many very friendly people. Then we went on to Sydney, Australia to attend the FIS Congress, representing the USA, and chairing the FIS ski jumping committee for the last time. I retired from that committee at that time after 28 years as a member, the last 16 as chairman. My close friend Torbjorn Yggeseth from Norway took over the chairmanship. After the Congress we traveled to Fiji Islands, and had a wonderful, relaxing time including 3 days on the Blue Lagoon Cruise.

There was exciting news when they arrived home. "After a short rest at home we drove to Butte, MT to visit Lou Ann as she had moved from Helena to a new job in a Butte television company. She also had a serious boyfriend, John Harris." The only thing that tempered the happiness was the death of Claire's mother soon after.

There were numerous trips to Norway. On one of them, Gus was the Technical Delegate from the FIS to oversee the World Ski Jumping Championships held in Holmenkollen. What a glorious moment to be back where his illustrious sporting career began. An extra added bonus was meeting his nephew, Fred Raaum. After another sojourn to Norway, back home…Dave and Georgia presented Claire & Gus with their first grandchild, Jennifer, born on 8/25/1982. In March of 1983, Chris and Joanie gave them another granddaughter, Allison. Altogether, there would eventually be six Raaum grandchildren. As the family grew, so did Claire and Gus's happiness. All the hard work was paying off in so many ways.

Chapter 38
Life Is Good

The beginning of 1984 started in a wonderful way. First, with a marvelous winter vacation. "All ten of us including 2 grandchildren went to Jackson Hole for a ski vacation for 9 days. We had great weather, snow and skiing conditions." In April, it was off to Hawaii for two weeks. Then, in July, the biggest family event of the year:

> We traveled to Bigfork, Montana for Lou Ann and John's wedding at Flathead Lake Lodge, July 8, 1984. Both the ceremony and the reception were held outside with Flathead Lake and Rocky Mountains in the background in brilliant sunshine, followed by a full moon. Some 70 guests joined the festivities with champagne, kransekake, dinner and a fine dance band. Our minister Jim Dowdy officiated.

In August, Gus and Claire rented a house on Vashon Island, and had a glorious time with Chris, Joanie and their beautiful baby, Allison. As Gus remembered, the weather was superb. "We waterskied, swam, sailed, played tennis and golf and had bonfires in the evening." For a man who had left his birth family in Norway so many years ago, the family he and Claire created was the fabric of their life. They immersed themselves in their children's lives, but now there were grandchildren to celebrate.

Clearly Gus loved all his grandchildren equally, but much to his relief and pride, there would be a male heir to the Raaum name. Dave's wife gave birth to Erik. "On October 19, 1984 our first grandson was born securing the Raaum name for the next generation. We enjoyed our visit to San Jose to view this blond, blue eyed little Viking, and to get acquainted with 2 year old Jennifer."

In Gus's own words, "1985 was a great year," as he and Claire set out on another whirlwind trip…this time to the Far East:

> It started with a marvelous 18 day trip to Japan and Hong Kong in February. We were invited as guests by ski officials in Sapporo (Yoshiro Ito) Japan in conjunction with a World Cup jumping competition there. It was considered by us as a thank you for all the work, cooperation and consultation I had with Japanese ski people over many years including the 1972 Winter Olympic Games in Sapporo. We enjoyed their outstanding hospitality which is second to none anywhere. After 5 wonderful days in Sapporo we visited Tokyo, Kyoto and Nara where we learned about their ancient history, temples, and lots of old buildings and new ones. We found the Japanese polite, efficient, hardworking, clean, and indeed made us feel welcome everywhere. The trip on to Hong Kong was also interesting with a real exhibition of an incredible intense working society. No unemployment benefits; you either work or starve. We also took a bus trip to the Chinese border to take a look at familiar rice paddies

and fish farms across the border…a great place to shop as well.

That trip was followed by a trip to Vancouver BC to attend the International Ski Federation (FIS) Congress. This time it would be all play and no work for a change. "It was fun again to visit with old ski friends from all over the world, particularly since for the first time in 30 years I did not have responsibilities."

Gus was also thrilled to learn his brother, Dick, and his wife, Luci, were moving to Sequim, Washington. This sleepy little community is known as the Northwest's Banana Belt because it has less rainfall than the rest of the state. Dick and Lucy shared a wonderful life in Sequim, but sadly she has since passed away. Dick is still living in Sequim where he enjoys his books on tape, good meals and the company of his dearest friend, Connie.

That year was also momentous because it was Gus and Claire's 35th anniversary. They marked that year with the purchase of a cabin perched on the Case Inlet of Puget Sound in Allyn, Washington. (Settled in 1853, the town was named after Judge Frank Allyn of Tacoma.) This special place would be a family gathering place for decades to come. That year Gus recalled the first special event. "A family reunion took place at Allyn which provided us with a mixture of work and fun (fishing, crabbing, clam digging, picking oysters, swimming, boating and pickle ball matches)." Between family gatherings, Gus and Claire would spend many a long summer day relaxing in the sun, fishing and clamming. Claire especially enjoyed taking her skiff out on Allyn Bay to fish for the illusive sea-run Cutthroat trout.

As the year went on, the family grew, "Chris and Joanie presented us with another granddaughter, (Courtney) on September 23rd." This little girl would one day have two beautiful sons of her own. Her first born, Jackson, would be Gus's first great grandchild.

On Gus' 60th birthday, January 20, 1986, Claire threw a surprise birthday party for him. The theme was "This is Your Life." Many years later, Gus remembered it clearly, "Lots of laughs, food, drink and music." Shortly after that celebration, Gus and Claire attended another milestone, Sun Valley's 50th. "We saw many old ski friends. The US National Ski Hall of Fame also had a reunion at Sun Valley at that time, and it was a lot of fun to visit with many of my friends in that group."

That year also brought some sad new, too. Lou Ann's husband, John, lost his mother. Claire's sister Gen was diagnosed with lung cancer. Claire invited her to visit the cabin to rest. Then Gus and Claire had to say goodbye to their dog, Polly, who died at the age of 15.

Another trip took them over the border to Canada to visit the World's Fair. On that trip, Gus met someone who shared a bit of his history. "From there we traveled to a fishing camp on a lake where we caught a lot of trout (34). On that fishing trip we met another older Norwegian, a former ski jumper who had also worked on the Norwegian passenger ship Stavangerfjord (small world)." This was the same ship that Gus worked on as an assistant purser so many years before. It was also the ship that delivered him to the shores of the United States and into a new life in 1947. It is indeed a small world. The next international journey would be for an honor, and a trip down memory lane.

> Claire and I were again invited to come as Honorary guests to the German Austrian Ski Jumping World Cup. Right after Christmas we traveled to Germany, first Oberstdorf, then to Garmisch-Partenkirchen where we spent New Year's Eve, on to Innsbruck and then finish up in Bischofshofen…great hospitality. Then we headed for Norway to visit family and old ski friends and received wonderful hospitality. I even met the old nursemaid who took care of me and my brother when we were small, and I visited with my godfather Jacob Stiansen (over 90 years old) who taught me to sail and fish.

The next year, 1987, brought more family fun. Claire and Gus traveled to babysit their grandchildren Jennifer and Erik while their Mom and Dad went helicopter skiing in Canada. Hawaii was also on the calendar. "In April we enjoyed 2 great weeks in Hawaii with Dick and Luci; lots of sun, swimming, tennis, snorkeling, sailing, and too much food and drink."

A few months later, they headed out to their old stomping grounds. "In June we enjoyed a nice week in Montana with Lou Ann and John with some hiking and fly-fishing, and visiting with some old friends after our 8 years in Montana." This was followed by one of many more family reunions at the cabin in Allyn for lots of "…sailing, fishing, water skiing, golf, pickle ball and swimming." This was where Gus and Claire were happiest…among family doing outdoor activities.

The beach cabin at Allyn, Washington.

Chapter 39
Royal Friendships

The 1988 Winter Olympics took Gus to Calgary where he spent eight days as a leader of FIS seminars in ski jumping with officials from Japan, Canada and the US. While Gus was there, he met a jumper who would become famous for his lack of skill. "While at the jumping hill I ran into Eddie the Eagle, who was walking up the steps towards the take-off with his jumping skis on his shoulder. It was blowing hard. I asked him if he had planned on doing some jumping that day, and his response was maybe not. His eye glasses looked like the bottom of a coke bottle." Known for his thick glasses, Michael Edwards aka Eddie the Eagle was a British plasterer who made his name for *not* skiing or jumping well at the '88 Winter Games. But he captured the world's imagination with his tenacity. At the time he told the press, "In my case there are only two kinds of hope—Bob Hope and no hope."

While Gus was in Calgary, he said, "We had a great HK Assembly in Calgary with a great turn-out. We inducted quite a few new Aspirants including Crown Prince Harald of Norway." He also mentioned the HK earlier in his memoirs when he went to the Sun Valley 50th anniversary. "We also had a small HK gathering at Peter Andrews condominium when we took in several new Aspirants including Stein Eriksen, and Otto Lang. I was elected President of HK by the Founders: Sigmund Ruud, Einar Bergsland, Knut Gresvig, and Bjorn Kjellstrom."

Gus with Crown Prince Harald of Norway.

Most people have never heard of HK, but Gus did his own short history of this secret and very selective group. He called HK, "The world's most exclusive ski oriented friendship society." It's made up of men who are either competitive skiers, ski jumpers or have been in the ski business. The founders were three Norwegians and one Swede who got together in 1943. Sigmund Ruud was a former world ski jumping champion, and later a FIS official and sporting goods store owner. Einar Bergsland was also involved in sporting goods, a FIS official and organizer of the famous Holmenkollen ski jumping and cross country festival. Knut Gresvig was involved with Gresvig ski equipment worldwide. Bjorn Kjellstrom was the Swedish inventor of Silva compass.

Gus described the founders as, "Four great friends with great sense of humor." According to Gus, they sponsored assemblies/parties all over the world in conjunction with World Ski Championships, big international ski events, and during FIS Congresses in many different countries. Gus lists some of the locations: These assemblies have been held in Oslo, Norway; St. Moritz, Switzerland; Cortina, Italy; San Francisco, California; Vancouver, Canada; Sun Valley, Idaho; Seattle, Washington; Garmisch-Partenkirchen, Germany; Innsbruck, Austria; Planica, Slovenia; Calgary, Canada; Vail, Colorado; Montreux, Switzerland; Kongsberg, Norway; Lillehammer, Norway; Mittendorf-Kulm, Austria; Christchurch, New Zealand; Trondheim, Norway; Oberstdorf, Germany; and Lahti, Finland.

There are no members in HK, only those "aspiring" to be. There is a rather elaborate ceremony to bring in new aspirants. Beyond possessing a strong interest in the ski sport, Gus wrote they must have: "A great sense of humor, an eye and the respect for beautiful and charming ladies, a multi language ability, and in general have the true spirit of HK". Ski leaders from many countries have been invited to become

HK emblem

Aspirants, who continue as Aspirants the rest of their lives, unless they do not behave according to acceptable standards of HK, thus being removed from the rolls. New Aspirants are generally on probation for one year to see if they meet the expectations of the President. Since HK is a friendship type organization it is important to keep in touch. Special activities were organized in Oslo at Sigmund Ruud's home during Holmenkollen week, where they had ski jumping competitions, and speed skating competitions in addition to lots of excellent food and drinks.

Because of their ages, in 1986, the Founders, elected to retire and become consultants to a new HK Presidium (Board). They elected Gus as the new President with the mission to select his own Presidium. Gus selected Graham Anderson, former President of the U.S. Ski Assn., ski racer and FIS official, as Minister of Finance. Peter Andrews, a Canadian, was chosen as Secretary General. Andrews was a former FIS Council member and ski official. Torbjørn Yggeseth of Norway, a former world class ski jumping champion and present chairman of the FIS Jumping Committee was selected to join. Gus selected Räto Melcher of Switzerland who was former chairman of the FIS Alpine Committee. At that time, Melcher was the mayor of St. Moritz.

In February of 2003, a major HK assembly was organized in St. Moritz during the World Alpine Ski Championships. It was the

60th anniversary of this storied group. At that time, Gus stepped down and Torbjorn Yggeseth a champion ski jumper from Norway took the position of President of HK. Gus summed up what the job of the HK President is, and the mission of the group in the following excerpt: His responsibility will be to select the new members of the Presidium, and to carry on the spirit of the HK including honoring it's motto, *Don't get too serious*. In general, this HK organization is a BOYS WILL BE BOYS organization, which is very loosely organized, but within ski circles, considered to be the World's most exclusive ski oriented friendship Society.

In July of '88, Claire celebrated her 60th birthday. A big party was held at the beach place that included all the children and grandchildren plus 40 friends. It was a memorable day with a band and lots of dancing. Gus and Claire finished the month with a lovely sightseeing tour of the San Juan Islands.

That October, Claire and Gus took a cruise on Holland America to the western Caribbean with landings in Mexico, Jamaica, and Grand Cayman Island. As usual, they had a ton of fun, "We snorkeled, swam, played deck tennis, ping pong, and danced to great music. We saw much damage caused by tornadoes. After we got off the ship we visited Epcot Center." Their happiness upon their return was diminished, though, as Claire's sister, Gen was losing her battle with cancer.

During this time, Gus wrote about Claire's involvement with the Washington State Pioneers. This was clearly a lifelong mission for Claire. She loved studying her genealogy especially researching her family of pioneers who travelled across America in wagon trains. In 1988, as president of the Daughters of the Pioneers of Washington, Claire was in charge of a huge celebration for Washington State Pioneers 100th anniversary. She held the position of president for a number of years. Her enthusiasm and passion were contagious. She traveled throughout Washington State and even the Midwest with her son, Chris, who videotaped the journeys and marvelous historical discoveries.

Another wonderful family ski reunion in Jackson Hole began the year of 1989. The following month, Gus traveled to Vail, Colorado for the World Alpine Championships. While there, he said, "They had a very nice HK gathering at the home of Pepi Gramshammer." Gramshammer was an Austrian ski racer born in 1932 who began his sport at the ripe old age of ten. In 1960, he came to Sun Valley to race professionally. He would go on to be the winner of many international and professional ski races. He settled in Vail where he was considered a real treasure, and is listed in the Colorado Ski and Snowboard Hall of Fame.

In May, Gus and Claire traveled back East and had a wonderful 2 week automobile trip through six states: Massachusetts, Rhode

Island, Vermont, Connecticut, New Hampshire, and Maine. As always, they had a great vacation. "We enjoyed the many historical sites. We visited several old friends. Gary Allen and Art Brown took us sailing off the coast of Maine. We finished off the trip with 3 days in Boston."

From the bustling city of Boston, they were soon off to the mountains of Montana. While visiting their beloved daughter and her husband, they hiked and did some fly-fishing. It was always good to be back in Montana to simply enjoy the natural beauty and not have to worry about the resort business anymore. The next trip was solo for Gus as he headed up to Alaska to fish. "Our group together caught 21 nice king salmon averaging 25 lbs."

As Gus ended his notes about that year, there was a sad passage: "Claire's sister, Gen, passed away after a 3 year long fight with cancer."

Chapter 40
Joy & Loss

Family, friends and travel are the recurring themes throughout Gus's memoirs. The family once again began the new decade, 1990, with another "Great skiing reunion in Jackson Hole with children and grandchildren." Gus and Claire were great traveling companions… Two for the Road. In April he and Claire took a long road trip through Oregon and California where they visited their son Dave and his family. The drive continued to the Lawrence Welk Resort in San Diego. From there, it was on to the Grand Canyon, Las Vegas, through Death Valley, to Lake Tahoe and home.

Once back home, Gus was elected president of Mercer Island Rotary, and they went to Portland, Oregon to attend the Rotary International Convention with 21,000 other Rotarians from all over the world. Gus was at home wherever in the world he went. He loved mixing with all kinds of people. That July, in fact, his friend, Hank Isaacson of Isaacson Steel, invited Gus to an exclusive private place called the Bohemian Club in California. (Some of their honorary members were Richard Nixon and William Randolph Hearst.) Gus described the ten day excursion as, "A most interesting experience. Outstanding speakers and I met many well-known personalities: Henry Kissinger, explorer Bob Ballard (found the Titanic), Rockefeller, Art Linkletter."

That was the year to celebrate 40 years of marriage. Claire and Gus were just as in love as they had been the day they married. They continued to share their love of outdoor sports and recreation. They celebrated their anniversary with yet another trip, this time to the Kamloops Mountains in Canada for a week of trout fishing on the lake.

In addition to being President of the Daughters of the Pioneers of Washington, Claire became a new trustee of the Women's Washington University Club. This club was founded in 1914 to foster a union of university women who promote education, cultural and social activities. Claire enjoyed contributing her time and talent to worthy causes.

In January of '91, the year began with a trip to the 77th Rose Bowl game. That year it was the University of Washington playing Iowa. The Huskies defeated the Hawkeyes with a 46-34 victory. It was also the month for another ski family reunion in Jackson Hole. Unfortunately, Claire injured herself and was laid up for almost five months. Fortunately the summer family reunion at the beach cabin went better.

Gus took a solo trip in early August to Oslo to attend his goddaughter Ellen's, wedding. It was a quick turnaround after only four days there. Later in the months, he and Claire traveled to Scandinavia for another fabulous sojourn:

> We traveled to Norway and took the mail boat tour from Bergen to Kirkenes. We traveled with Buz and Helen Smith, Bob and Barbara Hampson, and Bob and Norma Corbett, had a great guided tour near the Russian border, then we took the plane over Tromso to Bodo where we stayed overnight. Then we took the train through the valley to Trondheim, where we met an old ski jumping friend Torbjorn Falkanger. Then we took the train on to Lillehammer, and stayed several days at Ersgaard B&B. Lillehammer was working hard on preparing for the 1994 Olympic Winter Games.

In January of '92, Gus had a reunion of a different kind; Ancient Skiers in Sun Valley. This place was so much a part of his history. Ancient Skiers is a community of 55+ who get together to celebrate the snow ski industry, athletes and beloved mountains. What better place to celebrate than Sun Valley. The group has more than 1,000 members from the Pacific Northwest who insist on enjoying the sport of skiing as they glide into their golden years.

That spring, there was another trip across the big pond.

> In March I headed to Norway to attend the 100th Anniversary of the famous Holmenkollen ski jump, and to renew old ski jumping acquaintances from years

past. We had a great HK assembly which included the King of Norway. I took a quick trip to Lillehammer to meet with Gonner Helene Enger who had agreed to rent us cabins at Skeikampen. Then I headed for Stockholm to visit with Fred Raaum and family, then on to Lund to visit Mette and her family.

There were a few more trips after that one: Hawaii and Jackson Hole. But the really big event of the year was on October 1st with the birth of Chris and Joanie's third daughter, Erika Maureen. It was Gus and Claire's fifth grandchild. This was followed by another great honor:

On October 9th, 1992, I was elected into the UW Husky Hall of Fame with a gathering on Friday evening. The next day I was the guest of Athletic Director Barbara Hedges during the Hall of Fame football game between University of Washington and Univ. of California. We were introduced on the field at half-time and I received my Hall of Fame ring.

There was one more international trip in '92. Gus and Claire went to London for two weeks. "We traveled to many places outside London. We visited Jack and Irene Christensen, Scott Raaum's family and some FIS friends."

As 1993 unfolded, there would be some joyous moments; a long planned trip with the family to Hawaii, and trip with friends back east, a friend's wedding in Montana. Gus commented, "This brought back memories of Lou Ann and John's wedding there some 9 years earlier."

But the overarching theme of 1993 was grief. Their son, Dave and his children suffered an unthinkable loss when Georgianna died on April 1st. Georgianna fought valiantly for eight months before she succumbed to cancer. She was not only a wonderful mother, but an inspiration to all who knew her. Claire and Gus traveled to San Jose one week each month to offer comfort and support to Dave, Jennifer and Erik. Later that year, Dave completed work on a home in Jackson Hole. That Christmas, Claire, Gus and other family members traveled to Jackson Hole to celebrate Christmas. It would be a time to join the Raaum family together with strength and love and hope for happier times ahead.

Chapter 41
Olympic Memories

The following year would hold a lifetime of memories. Gus decided the whole family would attend the 1994 XVIII Winter Olympics in Lillehammer, Norway. Lillehammer had won the bid in 1988 to host, beating out the U.S., Sweden and Bulgaria. That year was the first time the Games were on a different year than the Summer Olympics. Also, it was only the second winter event hosted in Norway after the 1952 Winter Olympics in Oslo (five years after Gus had left his homeland). This would truly be a momentous event on every level for Gus, his family and his country. It's best to read how Gus described the experience:

> 1994 was a real big deal as our children and spouses joined us in attending the 1994 Winter Olympic Games. We stayed in 2 log cabins at Skeikampen, north of Lillehammer. These belonged to Gønner Helene Enger. She was behind me in High School. We paid $ 20,000 for our 21 day stay. She spent the money to put in inside plumbing. It was very comfortable. We even had TV. We had a ball. I saw some friends, and we saw a lot of events. This was the first time having attending 6 previous Winter Olympics, that I had to buy tickets to get in. Helene had laid in some food for us, and had a nice reception with dinner when we arrive. We used the bus service to town every day.

In addition to all the events and excitement, Gus had a wonderful time with his HK fellows in fun. It's amazing to read about the *royal* company he kept. Gus recounts a night to remember:

> HK had a great assembly in the restaurant above the ski jumps. King Harald came and stayed all evening. The King was supposed to attend a dinner not far away, but had decided to stay with our HK group until the end. I told the King about the desire of the Swedish King to attend our HK assembly, but that we turned him down, which King Harald found very amusing. Close to midnight there were only about 8 of us left having some scotch. Torbjorn Yggeseth, Gunnar Sunde, Petter Ronningen (president of the Olympic Organizing Committee), King Harald, Bengt-Herman Nilsson (adjutant to the Swedish King, and the guy who tried to get us to admit the Swedish King) and me. I suddenly realized that the last bus from downtown to Skeikampen was leaving town in about ½ hour, so I asked Ronningen to get us a taxi, but none was available, so he called the police station and got them to come up with a paddy wagon to pick us up. King Harald had his own car and the driver had been sitting outside in the lobby all evening waiting for his departure. I said good night to the King who left. Later we all piled in to the paddy wagon, and started to head down, when we realized that the Swede was not in the car. We had to turn around and come back to the restaurant, and there next to gate, was the Swede just in a sports jacket, it must have been 15 below zero. He

had gone to the bathroom when we left. We all had way too much to drink. The police said they could not haul us any further than to the bus station, which worked fine. Except the Swede had forgotten his ID badge, and the bus driver would not let him on the bus. So I yelled to the bus driver to let him on, and some other Swedes also traveling to the hotel at Skeikampen paid for him. It was a great evening.

When remembering it all, Gus simply said, "The whole Olympic trip was a wonderful experience." To this day, his children have held that time in their hearts the same way.

The Raaum family at the 1994 Winter Olympics.

After the Olympics, it was home to golf, travel and celebration. Gus proudly told of a trip where Claire scored the elusive golfer's goal: "In August we had a great long weekend at Jack Miller's place in

Methow Valley with many other good friends. Claire got a hole-in-one at the short course down the road a ways." That year, Gus's brother, Dick, marked his 70th birthday. Gus arranged to have Dick's children flown in from Sweden, London and California. It was another, "Great celebration."

Claire and Gus were very involved with their grandchildren, and that summer they took Chris's daughters on one of their trips. This would be more of an educational journey south. "We took Allison and Courtney to Baker City to expose them to the Oregon Trail and its history." Because of Claire's intense interest in her own pioneer history, this was a wonderful experience for the four of them. The trail stretches 2,170 miles from east to west and was used as a large-wheeled wagon route that connected the Missouri River to valleys in Oregon. This passion for her past would be a part of the rest of Claire's life. She made enormous contributions of her time and talent to the Pioneer Association of Washington State and the Daughters of the Pioneers. When her granddaughter, Erika, was old enough, they would both dress in pioneer costumes and give educational presentations in the public schools. Her talented son, Chris, has documented on video much of his mother's pioneer roots which will always be a family treasure.

Their travels---far and wide--- continued until the end of the year.

In October we traveled with Gordon and Virginia Albright on a 2 week trip to Tahiti, Bora Bora and other Society Islands. This turned out to be a very interesting and pleasant trip. There was a whole different world out there some 4,000 miles from everywhere. In November we went on a Dixieland Cruise from San Pedro to Catalina Island, then on to Ensenada, Mexico, dancing all the time to some 14 different Dixieland bands, then we finished up with 2 days at the San Diego Jazz Festival. We finished off the year by spending Christmas in Jackson Hole enjoying skiing with all our grandchildren and their parents.

The New Year of 1995 began with more travel to Sun Valley to ski with, "Our Ancient Skiers friends." (Gus continued his loyalty to this group until the end of his life.) Both he and Claire faced some medical challenges, he wrote: In February I had a pacemaker installed to keep my heart from stopping. In March Claire had a very sophisticated gallbladder operation.

A joyful event took place soon after with a wedding celebration; Dave married the second love of his life, Patsy. (Gus and Claire also acquired their 6th grandchild, Patsy's son Christopher. Patsy, Dave and family lived in California for two years, and then moved to Jackson Hole in 1997). This celebration was followed by another international trip with two grandchildren. "In June/July we had a great trip to Norway with our two oldest granddaughters, Jennifer and Allison to expose them to life, food, friends, family and some culture there."

Later in July, they headed north. "We tried some salmon fishing in Canada with some friends. We did not have much luck catching salmon." But in September, they caught a momentous event. "We attended a nice reunion at Big Sky in Montana. This was the 25th anniversary of the founding of Big Sky. We had my first 3 employees there, Tim Prather, Lynne Poindexter, and Vonnie Cutler." It was a lovely time reminiscing about the early Big Sky days and seeing how far the resort had come. It was also a reminder of how fast the time had gone.

When they returned, a royal visitor graced the U.S. soil; the King and Queen of Norway. Gus and his longtime friend, Olav Ulland, greeted the royal couple at the Nordic Heritage Museum. They viewed a marvelous display of the ski jumping history of Norwegians and, of course, this included Gus's triumphant past. The visit was capped with a great evening event. "I had the honor to act as the Master of Ceremonies during the Royal dinner at the Sheraton Hotel with some 1,100 guests present for this occasion."

Chapter 42
Beyond 70 And Going Strong

A big milestone occurred in 1996 for the Raaum family; on January 26th Gus celebrated his 70th birthday at a place close to his heart. Gus was right at home and surrounded by a lot of love. Gus recalled, "The celebration at the Nordic Heritage Museum had an open bar, great Scandinavian food and dance music by "The Kings of Swing." It was a very successful party."

To mark his birthday, and his vitality, he and Claire headed off for Sun Valley to spend time with the Ancient Skiers. Gus's life still revolved around skiing and friends as they followed up with another ski related trip. "In February I headed for Kulm, Austria to the World Ski Flying Championships and also on Feb. 10th we had an HK Assembly in Bad Mittendorf. We inducted 2 new Aspirants, Franz Rappengluch, Germany, and Dietmar Hemerka, Austria."

That year, another milestone was moving to a house on Mercer Island with an amazing view. They filled their lovely northwest-style home with their beautiful Norwegian furniture and wonderful memories. They hosted many holidays and special events. Claire and Gus would live out the rest of their married life in their lovely Mercer Island home.

As was their way, the Raaums were constantly on the go that year. They took a trip with Elder Hostel in Sacramento that featured Dixieland Jazz and toured California gold rush towns. Then went to Canada for a Heli-Hiking tour that take hikers into remote wilderness for a real adventure high among mountain vistas. That October, they were back in Jackson Hole for more hiking and fishing on the spectacular Snake River. They went back down to Jackson Hole for Christmas and of course more skiing.

The beginning of the New Year of '97, they did their annual trip to Sun Valley to ski and socialize with the Ancient Skiers who were all young at heart. Soon after, it was another solo international adventure. "In February I traveled to Trondheim, Norway for the World Ski Jumping Championships, where we also had a fine HK Assembly on Feb. 23rd. New Aspirants inducted were Per Ottesen, Norway and Esa Klinga, Finland."

That spring, there was more sad news in the Raaum family, when Dick's wife passed away from cancer. Throughout this time, the family pulled together to mourn the loss of Luci. In that spirit, the whole family gathered at the beach cabin for family fellowship in July. In the latter part of the month, Gus introduced two more grandchildren to his homeland. "We traveled to Norway with Erik and Courtney for a 3 week trip to show them Grandpa's territory. The weather was gorgeous."

As the year closed, Gus and Claire decided to celebrate the biggest holiday with a new tradition. Gus wrote, "This year the whole family (minus Lou Ann & John) went to Hawaii for Christmas for the first time, it was a real change from the snow and cold in Jackson Hole." In the years ahead, this would become an intermittent tradition that would happen in other seasons. Hawaii would be one of the family's favorite places to gather for many years to come.

The next year, 1998, opened with a spectacular trip to Africa. Gus described a colorful journey filled with extraordinary sights and sounds.

> We traveled with Buz and Helen Smith. We especially enjoyed South Africa, it reminded us so much about Washington State. In Cape Town and Johannesburg we found some unsafe conditions for tourists. We visited Pretoria and Soweto where Nelson Mandela's home now is a museum. Then we headed by plane to Nairobi, Kenya and spent 10 most interesting days on Safari in several game reserves near Mt. Kilimanjaro, then we headed north to Mt. Kenya Safari Club for several days, then further north to Samburu National Preserve. The roads were terrible, we got stuck several times, and our drivers had to pay off local people before they would help getting us out of the ditch. Kids were begging for anything we would give them. They seem to be friendly, smiling in spite of extreme poverty.

The following spring, it was north to the Yukon Territory and Alaska. In the 2 weeks they were gone, they traveled by land and sea and rail. Gus wrote, "It was a mixture of cruise ship, small train to White Horse, then river boat on the Yukon River, then a motor coach to Fairbanks with daylight all night. Then we traveled by train to Denali National Park, but we did not see Mt. McKinley or anything else, since it was foggy and rainy, stayed overnight, then continued on the train to Anchorage."

That summer, they held a huge family reunion at the beach house. The guests of honor were Dick's daughter, Mette, and his granddaughter, Jenny, from Sweden. Fun revolved around sailing, swimming and great conversation. Also that summer, Claire celebrated her 70th birthday. Gus made sure it was memorable, "…with a marvelous 7 day boat trip with friends up and down Willamette and Snake River. We were on a sternwheeler all the way up to Lewiston and Clarkston passing through 8 locks each way, with Lewis and Clark history all the time." Gus finished out the summer with some fun out on the golf course. "In August I had a ball volunteering as a marshal at the PGA Championships at Sahallee Golf Course in Redmond, where the best 100 golfers in the world competed."

In the fall, they were off to the annual Jazz Festival in Sun Valley. The next stop was to Gillette, Wyoming. They were there to support their granddaughter, Jennifer, who was competing in the state high school girls swimming championships. No matter how far and wide Claire and Gus traveled, they always carved out time for the family. That meant several trips that year to Jackson Hole to see Dave and his family.

The dawn of 1999 found them back with the Ancient Skiers in Sun Valley. A few weeks later, Gus traveled solo.

> I traveled to Vail, Colorado during the World Alpine Ski Championships and to lead the HK Assembly there. HK Aspirant Pepi Gramshammer and his wife were wonderful hosts in their beautiful home. I stayed a few days in Gramshammer Lodge, then I shared a room with HK Aspirant Guttorm Berge, who had come from Norway. Later in February I traveled to Austria during the World Nordic Ski Championships. While there we had a great HK Assembly, which was sponsored by Franz Rappengluch. We inducted 3 new Aspirants, namely Ueli Forrer of Switzerland, Hugo Kassel, Austria and Christian Poley of Austria.

The rest of 1999 was filled with numerous excursions to visit family, golfing and time at the beach in the warmer months. But at the end of the summer, Claire and Gus took another exotic and international trek:

> In the middle of September we traveled to Greece and Turkey for 3 weeks. At the beginning we had 4 very

interesting days in Greece. We stayed in the Esperia Palace Hotel in Athens. We hired a chauffeur with a Mercedes Benz (found on the internet) who picked us up at the airport, took us to the hotel, and every day came to the hotel to pick us up and took us all around interesting spots near Athens. South of Athens we went to the Aegean Sea, where we went swimming. We traveled up to Delphi, visited impressive ruins, buildings and sites and even attended a concert under the stars at the Acropolis. Our chauffeur spoke good English and he did not smoke. Then we spent 15 wonderful days traveling almost 2,000 miles through Turkey. From Ankara down to the Mediterranean Sea, then up the West coast through Ephesus and Troy to Istanbul. There was only one other couple on the tour (a lot of people cancelled due to devastating earthquake) so we ate with the locals, even were welcomed into a private home where they cooked over a hole in the floor. Local children came in to visit. Then the host invited us into the basement to show off their pride and joy, a donkey, which does a lot of the work, pulling wagons, etc. There is an enormous amount of history in Turkey which is also covered in the Bible. Istanbul was incredible. We visited the major market with acres and acres of everything in the world for sale. People were friendly and polite. We felt very safe walking around the city.

The new millennium would bring more adventures and challenges for Gus and Claire. Now, both in their 70's they were still going strong. Their marriage was as solid as ever and about to hit the half century mark. What a gift to have found true love at an early age and have it last a lifetime.

Chapter 43
Full Circle

The new millennium began with the Raaum's traditional ski trip to Sun Valley with the Ancient Skiers. That was quickly followed by Gus taking another international jaunt by himself.

> In February I traveled to Norway and attended the World Ski Flying Championships. In addition I anchored the HK Assembly held in Kongsberg on Feb. 10th. Great turnout with 24 Aspirants present. Sverre Seeberg (president of the Norwegian Ski Assn.) was inducted as new Aspirant. We had a very special cocktail hour in the HK special room, then Petter Hugsted took us on a tour of the ski museum, then we all assembled in Kongehallen (King's Hall) for a cocktail, and Franz Rappengluch surprised us all with a with a cocktail glass which was etched with the HK emblem.

Gus's memoirs clearly showed with all their travels, his and Claire's feet hardly touched the ground. There were more trips that year to Palm Desert, "As guests of Corbett's, we played a lot of golf, and cards, and attended many cocktail parties and dinners." There was another week long trip to Hawaii with family. Then, a place where Gus always felt at home: "I traveled to Alaska for salmon fishing as the guests of Foushee, we pulled in quite a few halibut and salmon." But along with all the traveling, the best part of 2000 revolved around a momentous event:

> The highlight of this year was our 50th wedding anniversary, planned, organized, carried out and paid for by our 3 children at Nordic Heritage Museum; a full deal with the Kings of Swing. All our grandchildren were very busy greeting people at the door, and assigned table seats for everyone. Gunnar and Lisbeth Sunde came all the way from Norway to attend. There were 119 people seated for dinner. It was a fantastic evening.

The next year, 2001, would hold more travels and adventures. It would also be a year that would live in infamy for the United States and the rest of the world. But before that event, Claire and Gus were still living in a world where travel was open and considered safe, even though the places they visited had some risk.

> We then had an unforgettable trip to Egypt and Jordan with the University of Washington Alumni Group. We traveled by private plane. We stayed at a fine hotel outside Cairo right next to the pyramids, in fact, we played golf right next to the pyramids. We flew by private plane over to the Sinai Desert, and to the

Gus & Claire in Egypt, 2001.

> monastery and saw what they claimed to have been the burning bush from the Bible, and also near where Moses picked up the Ten Commandments on stones on

top of Mount Sinai. We later saw where Moses was buried on top of Mount Nebo. He never made it to the Promised Land. We then traveled to many of the famous graves along the Nile. Then we spent several days on a passenger boat cruising up the Nile River stopping at various famous spots along the way. Our boat had several armed guards on board to protect us. Then we traveled in to Jordan, we traveled all the way from the South end to the North end of Jordan. We stayed overnight in a fancy resort next to the Dead Sea. We went swimming in the Dead Sea. It was extremely salty, so we floated on the very top of the surface. Our original plans were also to visit Israel, but the political situation was very unstable and considered not safe, so we never went there.

In between this last trip and the next, were some other family celebrations. "In June we attended two high school graduations, one in Jackson, Wyoming for Jennifer, and then in Redmond for Allison. In July my nephew, Fred Raaum and family came to visit from Sweden. We had a Raaum reunion at the beach." A month later, Gus got a new pacemaker before he and Claire headed out on a two-week trek in Ireland. They were in Belfast on one of the saddest days in US history; September 11, 2001. Gus wrote:

> The Irish people were very understanding and expressed a lot of sympathy, they held special Mass in a huge cathedral in Knock in our "honor" attended by some 9,000 people. They hung American flags out their

windows. The whole country shut down one day in our "honor". Both Ireland and Northern Ireland people were very nice and friendly.

The warmth of the Irish people helped Gus and Claire through the rest of that sad time as they made their way home. Many things must have gone through their minds as they took off from the Emerald Isle. But one has to imagine that Gus realized he was first and foremost a true American citizen. This was the country that had given him so much. Two years after the tragedy, he would be deeply reminded again of his citizenship when he visited Manhattan to see his granddaughter, Jennifer. Among the places they visited were Ground Zero and Rockefeller Center. But the most profound moment came on the Staten Island Ferry. First, as they glided past Ellis Island, once the gateway for more than 12 million immigrants; and next, the Statue of Liberty, the greatest symbol of freedom.

As Gus gazed upon Lady Liberty, his mind wandered back nearly 60 years to the first time he saw it. He was a lad working as an assistant purser, standing on the deck of a Norwegian ship called the Stavangerfjord. At that time, he wrote, "I ran up to the bridge of the ship to watch as we passed the Statue of Liberty." After that initial trip across the Atlantic, Gus returned to Norway; little did he know that someday America would become his home…the land of *his* opportunity.

The Final Jump

Gus ended his personal writings in 2003. The last decade of his life was filled with more traveling, golfing and family time. But it was also a time of great loss when his beloved Claire passed away on February 5, 2013. The following recollections are compiled from his three children as they recalled the final years of Gus's life.

Dave recalled how Gus and Claire were always willing to travel to family events especially for their grandchildren's' milestones. Dave listed the following: Erik's graduation from Jackson Hole High School (2003); Jennifer's New York University commencement (2005); Christopher's graduation from the University of Utah (2007), and Erik from University of San Diego (2007). Dave fondly recalled many wonderful family excursions to Hawaii, another place Gus and Claire thoroughly enjoyed. Throughout that last decade, Dave, Patsy and their children made many memories with the senior Raaums at the beach cabin and Mercer Island. Whenever it was possible, they'd visit during the Christmas holidays.

For Dave, some of his fondest recollections focused on the many trips that he and his wife, Patsy, took to the Sun Valley Jazz Festival with Gus and Claire. For four years in a row (2008-2011), they attended this wonderful event in Sun Valley, a place where Gus and Claire had spent so many happy days on the ski slopes. By 2012,

Claire was not well enough to travel to Sun Valley one last time. Gus considered attending in the next two years, but he knew it just wouldn't be the same without his beloved Claire. Dave said this about their last trip, "Mom and Dad traveled to Salt Lake City in August 2012 to attend grandson Christopher Johnston and Sara's wedding. This was their last trip before Mom was diagnosed with cancer."

After Claire was diagnosed, Dave and Patsy would visit Mercer Island as frequently as they could to offer comfort and support. After Claire passed, a few months later, they would help Gus move to his new home at Covenant Shores. In August of 2014, Dave fondly remembered a car trip he and Patsy took with Gus:

> We went to Sequim to visit his brother Dick. Patsy met her older brother Ray for the first time that day at Port Townsend. The next day was Ray's 70th birthday, so he invited us to his friend's house on Dabob Bay. Dad went with Patsy and I, and it was a grueling 5-hour drive and ferry ride due to heavy traffic. Even so, Dad thoroughly enjoyed himself. We had an excellent seafood lunch at Ray's friend's house, walked down to the beach, and visited. We were exhausted when we finally got back to Covenant Shores, but Dad was a real trooper.

Gus would spend about 18 months living at Covenant Shores, an assisted living facility. Dave was often present, even though he lived far away. Dave recalled, "During all of these trips and visits, Dad never complained about his chemotherapy treatments that were very toxic. He had some severe side effects, but always kept a positive attitude." Dave continued to say:

> He had many Mercer Island friends already living at Covenant Shores, so it was an easy transition. The whole family helped get the Mercer Island house ready to sell, and helped him move into his new condominium at Covenant Shores. During the year and a half that he lived there, Chris visited him almost every day, so he was well taken care of. I logged into his computer every month to help him balance his bank accounts and credit card. It couldn't have been easy to acknowledge that he needed help, since he was a CPA, but he was very realistic about it. He always looked forward to that call on the first of every month.

Throughout this time, Gus always kept in touch with his brother, Dick. They would chat regularly by phone speaking some times in their native tongue. Dave was thrilled when Dick and his son made a final visit to Gus. Dave said, "Dick's son Scott drove Dick down from Sequim to Covenant Shores for a final visit just before Dad passed away. They spoke both English and Norwegian and enjoyed each other's company for the last time."

For Chris, so many memories were filled with marvelous holidays together whether it was at their home or with his Mom and Dad on Mercer Island. Family vacations were often spent at the cozy beach cabin or as far away as Maui. Even though it was so difficult for Gus to go the Hawaii without Claire, he still joined the extended family for his last trip there in May of 2014.

Since Chris lived the closest to his dad, he was able to spend more time with him, whether it was at Husky football games or eating meals with him at Covenant Shores. Chris admired how Gus handled his own cancer diagnosis which he survived for more than a decade. Chris said, "He always stayed positive, even in the infusion rooms, and willing to help others who were there." This was the same attitude that had gotten Gus through all of his life…through the best and the worst.

Chris has fond memories of a trip he and his dad took to Norway in February 2011 to the Nordic World Championships in Oslo. What stands out is the time he and Gus spent with King Harald V of Norway. Chris was particularly impressed by Harald's genuine kindness and by the respect he had for Gus. When it was time to take a picture with the King, he insisted that Gus be front and center.

Chris and Gus visited the Holmenkollen Ski Museum to see all his honors and memorabilia. They even found a picture of Gus with the King hanging on the wall of a restaurant. Someone made a joke that they recognized Gus in the photo but, "...didn't know the guy next to him!"

Gus & Chris with King Harald V of Norway.

They rode the trains throughout Norway taking a trip down memory lane. Everywhere they went, Gus was recognized as a national hero. Even after several decades, he visited the Lillehammer ski club and was immediately applauded. (Chris recalled when Gus had gone over for the winter Olympics on a previous trip, he was front page news.) It would be Gus's last trip to his homeland, and today Chris holds treasured memories of a magical time.

When Gus faced his own demise, he stayed cheerful until the very end. All of the family surrounded him as his time drew near. Chris said, on that day---December 28, 2014---the Seahawks had a play-off game. When the family stepped out of the room for a few moments to watch the kick-off, Gus slipped the bonds of earth. One has to wonder if he felt himself soar above it all, just like that glorious ski jump in 1946 when he made history.

When asked about her favorite memories of her Dad, Lou Ann and her husband John had many wonderful recollections about visits to Mercer Island and the beach cabin. as well as trips together to Norway and Maui. But for Lou Ann, a visit by Gus to Bozeman in July 2014 really stands out. It's best to read about it in her words:

> I arranged for Dad to fly over to Bozeman for a short visit that summer. When he arrived, the first thing he said was, "I would love to go fly-fishing". So we booked a half-day float on the Yellowstone River. He absolutely loved it and caught some beautiful trout. It was also the first time that he and I had gone fishing together, since I had just taken up fly-fishing in recent years. It was a wonderful time spent together, and it is a somewhat bittersweet memory because he passed away 6 months later.

Gustav will forever be remembered as "The Viking." In fact, Chris recalled that his brother Dick was nicknamed "Viking North" and Gus was "Viking South." But beyond the championships, honors and professional accomplishments, he'll be revered for so much more. Gus was a faithful and loving husband. Claire would always be that beautiful, feisty UW co-ed who swept him off his feet. Together, they raised a family and traveled the world. He stayed by her side until her last breath, and life would never be same after that. But even with a hole in his heart, he always showed up for his children and grandchildren. As did Claire, he doted on all his grandchildren. Gus was blessed to be alive when his first great-grandchild, Jackson, arrived.

For Gus Raaum, it was definitely a life well lived. As a tenacious young man who survived a world war and went on to make sports history. As a young immigrant who was determined to get an education and seek the American dream. As a husband and father who put family first. A Hebrew proverb says it best: *Say not in grief he is no more - but live in thankfulness that he was.* That thankfulness is still felt in those who knew and loved him. As for Gus's gratitude, he lived by his own personal motto: "Every day is a good day." And those good days added up to one great life!

Addendum

Gus & Dick with their nanny, Ruth Johnson.

Gus jumping at Lysgardsbakken, 1945.

The 4-way jump in Sun Valley, 1948. Gus is 2nd from left.

Some of Gus's trophies from 1948-1949.

An early Raaum family photo, 1963.

Crystal Mountain Ski School, 1966.

Visiting Bedouins during 1967 FIS Congress in Beirut.

Gus with his grandchildren Erik, Jennifer, Courtney & Allison.

Gus overseeing the ski jumping at the 1980 Lake Placid Olympics.

Hopprenn yngste klasse. 15 premier.

1. Gustav Raaum, Lillehammer skikl. 227.60
2. Hugo Persson, Bærum Skikl. 224.20
3. Christian Mohn, Heming 221.50
4. Sigurd Olsen, Str. & L.str. 219.30
5. Hans Bjørnstad, Drafn, Drammen 217.80
6. Sverre Kronvoll, S. Land I.L. 217.10
7. Øivind Mastermo, Mo i Rana 216.90
8. Per Gjelten, Freidig, Trondheim 216.70
9. Bengt Jäderholm, Sverige 215.50
10. Hans Ludvik Dehli, Stabekk I.F. 215.10
11. Odd Winquist, Lillehammer Skikl. 214.90
12. Claus Dahl, Ready, Oslo 214.70
13. Alf Løcka, Kongsberg idr.f. 214.60
14. Sverre Lie, Nordstrand I.F. 213.70
15. Asbjørn Sørlund, Rena I.F. 212.20
16. Gunnar Hagen, Lena I.L. 208.90
17. Thorbjørn Berntsen, Nydalen Skikl. 208.70
18. Alf Børresen, Koppang I.F. 207.40
19. Odd Løberg, Hamar I.L. 207.20
20. Sverre Stalvik, Byåsen I.L. 206.90
21. Birger Arnesen, Slemmestad sp.kl. 206.60
22. Kjell Knarvik, Mysen I.F. 204.70
23. Per Hanevold, Asker Skikl. 204.60
24. Ivar Grønberg, Tistedalen Turn & I.F. 202.10
25. Arne Dahlby, Åmot I.L. 200.00
26. Odvar Laskogen, Lena I.L. 196.20

Placings in the Under 20 Class, 1946 Holmenkollen.

Nordic Festival Report - 1965

298

Record of Gus's birth, 1926 (in Norwegian).

Gus & Claire's marriage certificate, 1950.

Gus's Certificate of Naturalization.

Gus's 1946 Holmenkollen trophy.

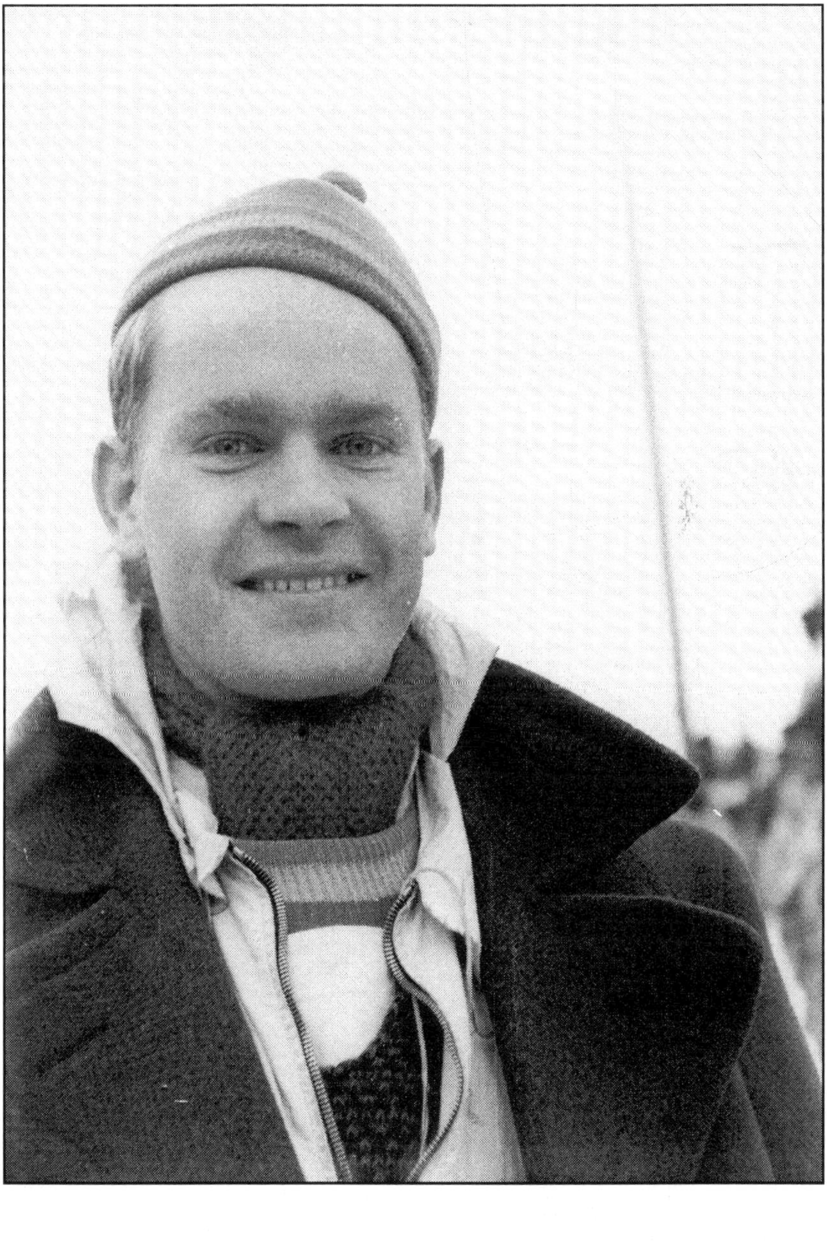

Made in the USA
Lexington, KY
16 November 2017